LIFE:
JESUS-STYLE
Scaling the Sermon on the Mount

by James Long

VICTOR BOOKS

a division of SP Publications, Inc.
WHEATON. ILLINOIS 60187

Offices also in Fullerton, California • Whitby, Ontario, Canada • Amersham-on-the-Hill, Bucks, England

Fourth printing, 1981

Bible quotations are from the *New American Standard Bible,* copyright 1960, 1962, 1963, 1968, 1971, 1972, 1973, The Lockman Foundation, La Habra, California.

Library of Congress Catalog Card Number: 78-058692

VICTOR BOOKS
A division of SP Publications, Inc.
P.O. Box 1825 ● Wheaton, Ill. 60187

Contents

*Thank You, Lord, for Harriet,
a challenge and example to me of
life, Jesus-style*

1

My Feet Are Firm
on This Here Sod

I don't know if I should own up to this or not, but 'tis true:

I have this thing about Gospel songs and hymns—nothing wrong with the songs—but I hear them and, for some reason, *other words* squeeze into my mind.

Perhaps you know the chorus that goes:

> *I've got a home in glory land*
> *that outshines the sun. . .*
> *Away beyond the blue.*

One evening I was picking around on my 12-string guitar, playing that tune. The words were buzzing in my head. But all of a sudden, these words hit me:

> *I've got a home in glory land*
> *But my feet are firm on this here sod,*
> *Dear God!*

Believe me, there was no sacrilegious intent. To the contrary, something stung my conscience. It is very easy to sing about our "home beyond the blue," but it's not so easy to live as if we really have one!

I think, for instance, of one of my worst attempts at "witnessing." I was playing in a band at the time and we were rehearsing. Between songs I leaned across my drums and invited our two guitar players to come to church with me the next day, Sunday. Simultaneously, right on cue, both laughed, and one said, "If *you* are a Christian, I don't think I want to!"

He said it jokingly. And I knew how he meant it. But I still felt like throwing my drumsticks his way. Problem? I was not consistent. I was not living life, Jesus-style. My attitudes were wrong. All of that showed. It shined like a city on a hill— the wrong city, the wrong hill.

Which Brings Us to Matthew, Who Brings Us to Jesus

The first time I read the Sermon on the Mount in Matthew 5—7 I was shocked! The concepts Jesus shares are radical. It's His special talk on attitudes, character, values. What He presents as *His* style of life stands in stark contrast to commonly accepted guidelines for life.

And it occurs to me that I am not the first to be shocked by what He says there. Matthew reported, "The result was that when Jesus had finished these words, the multitudes were amazed at His teaching; for He was teaching them as one having authority, and not as their scribes" (7:28-29).

But what did He say that surprised them?

Well, for starters He said, "Blessed. . ." Nine times He said, "Blessed" (5:3-11).

Now you know He didn't just pronounce nine "blesseds" and move on to another topic. He said something special about each of the nine. He

OUR IDEA OF WHAT WILL MAKE US HAPPY DOES NOT ALWAYS AGREE WITH GOD'S IDEA OF WHAT _SHOULD_ MAKE US HAPPY.

ACCEPTING THAT FACT IS LIKE SWALLOWING A FOOTBALL SIDEWAYS!

A BITTER PILL INDEED.

pointed out that deep-and-wide happiness goes along with some special attitudes and character traits. It's not surprising that He held His audience's attention. We're all interested in happiness.

Call it "blessedness" if you wish.

The snag in all this is that our idea of what will make us happy—bless our souls—does not always agree with His. Accepting that fact is like swallowing a football sideways—a bitter pill indeed.

Take Jonah for Example

When it came down to the wire, Jonah offered noodle commitment—just a lot of soggy excuses. As a result, his failure became a feature in God's Book, four chapters worth.

You should digest it.

But don't duplicate it!

Rebellious and unwilling "prophets" are still spreading Jonah-style heartburn from their weak responses, in epidemic proportions. You can imagine the upheaval *that* creates!

Ask the fish!

Or ask Jonah.

I see the moral of the story emerging: Jonah gets these vibrations, "Go to Nineveh! Tell it like it is! Go, Jonah, go!"

So Jonah says to himself, *I know what them there Assyrians are like. And if I am to be an individual who is happy and blessed, I shan't go to Nineveh. Methinks I will board the next jet out of Joppa. I shall take off for Tarshish!"*

Happy. . .

Blessed. . .

It's all in how you look at life. That's what makes the Sermon on the Mount so astounding. It is a different look, bringing heaven down to earth. Life, Jesus-style.

The Hypocrites Ain't Blessed

I once sat in a Sunday School class, entranced by the teacher. (I was quite young.) He was active and influential in the church. But he left his wife and kids for someone else.

I tucked that memory away in a special place in my mind so that later, when I heard the word "hypocrite," I would be able to define it and use it in a sentence.

Over the years (that makes me sound quite elderly) I have compiled quite a list of hypocrites. One afternoon I stood on the pier at Seal Beach in California talking to a middle-aged, beet-red fisherman.

Hmmm, I said to myself, *this man needs the Gospel. Probably.*

I didn't get very far into my presentation before this kindly gentleman interrupted me. "I want to tell you something," he said.

"Oh?" says I "What's that?"

He talked to me for 20 or 30 minutes, explaining his spiritual experience. He and his wife had made professions of faith. They had become active in a small church. They spent a lot of time visiting in the homes of other leaders in the church.

Then his wife became sick, was hospitalized, and suffered with cancer for nearly a year. "Not once," he told me, "did any of those church friends even come or call. Then one day my wife died, and the church sent flowers."

And the church sent flowers!

He had a longer list of hypocrites than I did. He had the membership role of an entire church.

Just before he turned and walked away he said, "Don't talk to me about Christianity."

I think about that man from time to time. When I do I visualize his bright red face, his bushy white hair, and an assortment of wilting flowers.

Well, the hypocrites are not blessed. But neither are the people who use them as an excuse for less than total commitment to Jesus.

What About the Spiritual Superstars?

Paul always impressed me as a supersaint; so did John, and Peter—yes, Peter! Bartholomew did too (when I finally learned how to spell his name). Pastors, missionaries, youth directors, and scoutmasters also seemed to shine as spiritual superstars.

There is something pretty comfortable about all of this categorizing. If you do everything just right, you can leave yourself out without feeling guilty.

Let's suppose, for any one of a number of poor reasons, you feel a bit unspiritual and inferior. At the same time you hear all of these sermons and you just can't get it all together. What do you do? You tell yourself, *I may not be as good as the Apostle Paul, but at least I'm not as bad as Judas Iscariot!*

As long as we are comparing ourselves with other *people* we can swing it so we look OK. We just get selective about who we compare ourselves with.

Meanwhile, back to the hypocrite question:

What really goes on inside our minds when we are hiding behind some other person's sin?

What a creep! Even I am better than that!

Or, if *you* happen to feel like the creepy one, you

can either find somebody creepier, or you can
compare yourself with some sterling silver saint.

> *I'm doing my best. Of course I can never
> make it! Look at the competition! God
> doesn't expect much of me. I'm not
> equipped like the apostles! Or my youth
> director. Or Mom.*

Paul told the Corinthians, who were apparently
tuned to this frequency, that all this comparing
ourselves with others is stupid—unwise
(2 Corinthians 10:12).

So we spend a lot of time hiding behind the
biggies or the smallies, manufacturing our own
standards of measure. But Matthew says, "Hey!
How about life, Jesus-style?"

Back to the Blesseds

I'm thinking again about the nine blesseds in
Matthew 5. And I have some questions. Jesus
talks about:

    people who are poor in spirit,
    people who mourn,
    people who are gentle,
    people who are hungry and thirsty for righ-
        teousness,
    people who are merciful,
    people who are pure in heart,
    people who are peacemakers,
    people who have been persecuted for the sake of
        righteousness.

These people are living life, Jesus-style. And they
are happy people.

But would you put happiness and spiritual poverty together? Would you think of poor in spirit
with a smile on it?

If you place happiness and mourning in the

same circle they seem to push each other out. One wins. They can't coexist. Or can they?

And if you put "gentleness" or "meekness" on a word association test, would you get "blessed" or "happy" in response? Maybe you'd get "pansy," or "likely to be ripped-off."

What is your image of a person who is "hungry for righteousness"? Does he have a smile? Or is he somber?

"Mercy" seems to be such a serious word. We tend to think of it in some austere, judicial setting. A kind judge—"Thirty days! Instead of six years." A lighter sentence.

"Purity of heart." Is it for prudes and people too old to know the difference? Or is purity really a thing of joy?

When you read "peacemaker" do you see a determined lawyer? A union negotiator? A mother standing between her two sons? Or what? Are they happy?

"Blessed are those who have been persecuted for the sake of righteousness." Do happiness and persecution belong together?

And Jesus makes it even more personal when He adds number nine: "Blessed are *you* when men revile you, and persecute you, and say all kinds of evil against you falsely, on account of Me. Rejoice, and be glad, for your reward in heaven is great" (5:11-12).

Heaven is to be the reference point for all of our values. Let's bring heaven down to earth. Life, Jesus-style.

The Opposites, Not Attractive

I remember reading Matthew 5 and gliding right over all nine of those "blesseds." When a friend took the time to explain them, I realized I'd been gliding over them in my manner of living as well.

My friend explained them to me by talking about their opposites. When I saw the opposite characteristics in my life, I knew I had been nailed

The Blesseds	Their Opposites
Poor in Spirit	Attitude of Pride
Mourn	Insensitive
Gentle	Angry, Greedy
Hunger for Righteousness	Indifferent
Merciful	Bitter, Resentful
Pure in Heart	Impure Thoughts
Peacemaker	Critical, Judgmental
Persecuted	Ashamed of God

In one afternoon, during the two-hour discussion in which my friend shared these concepts, I saw I had hurt my testimony as a Christian with my parents, my brother, my friends. I had a small glimpse of life, Jesus-style.

Salt Without Savor

Have you ever noticed how easy it is to misunderstand something? I used to read that there would be "earthquakes in divers places" (Matthew 24:7, KJV), and I visualized scuba divers getting all shook up, their masks cracking and their regulators malfunctioning. I guess I was a bit relieved to discover that "divers" meant "various." Having been raised in Southern California, I have always been partial to the sea.

Similar problem: I used to read Matthew 5:13, "But if the salt have lost his savor . . ." (KJV), and wonder, *What on earth is 'savor'? How did this salt get it? Is it anything like being iodized?*

Another King James-related mystery was solved when I saw a menu that referred to a hamburger as "savory."

Oh yes, "savor," as in "savory." "If the salt loses its taste."

And just what is tasteless salt? I ask myself.

Myself answers, *Tasteless salt is worthless salt.*

Jesus said, "You are the salt of the earth; but if the salt has become tasteless, how will it be made salty again? It is good for nothing any more, except to be thrown out and trampled underfoot by men" (5:13, NASB).

He's talking about Christians without zing.

Salt was used for three things in Jesus' day. It was used for seasoning, that we understand. It was used in some of the Jews' religious ceremonies associated with certain offerings. And it was used so food wouldn't decay so quickly.

The person who lives life, Jesus-style, has a responsibility to get shaking, to touch everything he can with that good flavor of Jesus-style living. As bland and decaying as our world is, people are quick to taste the difference.

Glance back at that list of characteristics (the Beatitudes) and their opposites. The left column is full-flavor saltiness; the one on the right is salt without savor.

There are people all over the place on spiritually salt-free diets. Shake! Give them a taste of life, Jesus-style.

Light Outasight

My family often drove from Southern California to Kansas where my relatives lived. Many of those trips were made "straight through," switching off on the drivers. Whenever we took "the Southern Route," Route 66, it seemed we always hit Albuquerque, New Mexico, at night.

There is always something about the open country of New Mexico that makes a black night seem blacker. As the odometer clicks off the miles, and with your eyes on the horizon, you can tell you are approaching Albuquerque long before you get there. The lights of the city can't be hidden.

Living life, Jesus-style, means that we share His character; we are like Him. As different as light is from darkness, so our lives should stand out in the world.

"You are the light of the world." Jesus says so in His Sermon (5:14). "A city set on a hill cannot be hidden. Nor do men light a lamp, and put it under the peck-measure, but on the lampstand; and it gives light to all who are in the house. Let your light shine before men in such a way that they may see your good works, and glorify your Father who is in heaven" (5:14-16).

There is no point in being a loose light bulb, giving the outward appearance of being a light but never sending out one ray. Dark "light" is as useless as salt without savor. It's absurd. Perhaps that's why Jesus uses these illustrations—light of the world, salt of the earth. The point can hardly be missed.

2

Reach for the Stars!

I still remember the way our old '56 Chevy station
wagon jerked when my brother downshifted into
second gear as we snaked our way up the side of
the Sierra Nevada Mountains in Northern
California. Destination: Dinky Creek, where
years earlier we had gone to church camp.

Before I tell you about Dinky Creek, I must
make you appreciate what our turquoise and
white, six-cylinder Chevy was going through.
Early that morning my brother and I had loaded
that thing like you would not believe—sleeping
bags, pots, pans, lantern, ice chest—and we
headed for Dinky Creek.

As we started up that mountain road, cornering
the treacherous switchbacks, skillfully missing
those heavily loaded logging trucks, we felt like
the Dynamic Duo, winning the West, blazing
trails, and all the rest.

As those logging trucks descended the slopes at
a threatening pace, the dust swirling around our
Baby Moon hubcaps, we were *ascending*. Slowly.
When third gear protested, my brother depressed
the clutch with his left foot, shoved the gear shift
into second, and popped the clutch. When he did,

all the junk in the back of that tired Chevy shifted with an unnerving crunch.

As the mountain road began to level off and we related our maps to our location, we found that we were indeed returning, like the swallows of Capistrano, to Dinky Creek.

Pinecone Promises

My first experience at Dinky Creek was in August, 1963 when, as a junior high school graduate anticipating my first year of high school, I attended a church camp for the first time. It was incredible.

I made some great friends. But the good times were interrupted by what I considered at the time to be extended slices of boredom. The counselors called these "classes."

I felt rather restricted, surrounded by some of the most beautiful country in the United States, yet corralled by a rigid schedule of classes and organized recreation.

Friday afternoon was beautiful—thunder, lightning, rain, and hail. Two outdoor meetings had been scheduled for that evening. The first was canceled. But the sky cleared in time for the climax of the week: a fireside testimony service.

Interesting footnote: Unwilling to have wet firewood dampen their spirits, the counseling staff used gasoline to start the campfire.

As a young non-Christian, my first reaction to the teary testimonies was, *Is this for real?* But an hour or so later I stood before my peers with a pinecone in my hand, ready to toss it in the fire as I said, "I have not been the kind of Christian I should be."

I heard a girl say that about three pinecones

earlier. The truth was, I was not a Christian at all. There were two very important things going on in my mind that motivated me to walk up to that fire and make my one-sentence speech:

(1) It was the thing to do.

(2) I was getting very cold sitting on a log in the back row.

But I must admit I did try to clean up my life a bit after that.

Then several years later my brother and I decided to take a one-week camping trip in the Sierras, 300 miles from home, and we wound up at Dinky Creek.

As darkness fell that evening, we built a small campfire, talked a lot, and read several chapters from the Gospel of Matthew. As we were reading, some amazing things were beginning to rattle around in my brain.

Through Matthew's Gospel I was beginning to see that Jesus Christ had already done for me what I'd been unable to do for myself. My values were being challenged. Slowly, terribly slowly, my life was beginning to change.

And Dinky Creek had played a big part in that change.

So did Matthew's Gospel.

King on the Mountain

The question once occurred to me, why *four* Gospels? Why not *eleven,* one written by each of the faithful disciples? You know, equal time. Or, why not *one?* Save on ink, paper, and printing costs. Bibles, after all, are among the most expensive books you can buy.

I have been told that each of the four Gospels presents Jesus Christ from a slightly different perspective—four witnesses to His life. John emphasizes the Deity of Jesus. Luke presents Him as the ideal, perfect man. Mark stresses the servanthood of Christ—moving dynamically in history; meeting human needs.

But in a unique way, Matthew introduces us to Jesus the Messiah, the King. It is in that position of King that Jesus sat down on the mountainside with His disciples to talk about His kingdom (5:1).

Campaign Promises, Our National Sport

We're all acquainted with political campaign promises. You know how it is. The person stands in front of 31 microphones, smiles at the TV cameras, kisses a few babies, and tells the nation, "If elected I will put an end to the common cold!" (Cheers.)

His opponent, not willing to be so easily trounced, upstages him by promising to abolish all types of flu. (Cheers and whistles.)

Since the people who listen to the candidates tend to have a harder time with flu than with colds, you know which one has the edge. But the person who ultimately gets the votes is the one who, up to the last minute of the campaign, can do the best job convincing the people that he can deliver the goods.

And ship out the bads.

It's like the candidate for high school student body president who promises, if elected, he will do away with history classes, extend lunch to three and a half hours, and fire the principal.

Most of us do not really believe campaign promises, but we enjoy hearing them. It's part of our culture. The more discontent we are, the more we enjoy the game—Political Wishful Thinking.

Things have not changed a whole lot over the centuries.

In Jesus' day the Jews were looking for a miracle-working Messiah who would end their hassles with Rome, and see that they got fresh bread, daily. I imagine that's why the Lord's followers were so unsettled.

He walks on water.

Great! Make Him king!

He speaks of coming persecution.

Hmmm. Don't know if I like that.

He turns water to wine.

Bravo!

He says, "Take up your cross."

I'm not sure that's what I signed up for.

This controversy ran through His entire three-year ministry and can be detected in this Sermon He preached so early in His ministry.

In those first few verses of Matthew 5 it's all the same; we've seen it before:

The poor in spirit get the kingdom of heaven.

The mourners are comforted.

The gentle inherit.

The people who are hungry for righteousness are filled.

The merciful receive mercy.

The pure in heart see God.

The peacemakers are called sons of God.

The ones who are persecuted get the kingdom of heaven.

These do not sound like the words of an all-powerful king, but they are certainly the words of a Person who is sure He *will* reign as King. In the Sermon on the Mount, Jesus the King clearly outlines the character traits of those who are His followers.

And the standards are high.

The Yoke's on You

I was sprawled across the living room floor watching a Grade B western. The Indians spoke with Brooklyn accents. The cowboys overworked words like, "hombre," "podna," and "Much obliged, Ma'am." As they rode across the sage I could see, if I looked carefully, telephone wires in the background, or a car on a distant paved highway, and on rare occasions, the vapor trail of a jet in the sky.

I took another handful of popcorn and chuckled to myself when they got to the part where the cowpoke looks as though he's trying to decide, *Do I kiss the girl, or the horse?* Sometimes a tough decision for him.

Then the station broke away for a few commercial messages. A familiar face smiled from the TV. It's "Honest Sharky" the used-car salesman. He kicks the tires, pounds on the hood, tells how low the mileage is, and suggests a price.

Every generation has its con artists. First-century Israel was no exception! In my mind's eye (wherever *that* is) I can see this guy—"Honest Irving"—in a white tunic selling yokes—the kind they harnessed oxen to.

This man is explaining how you'll get more mileage out of your oxen if you'll just hook 'em up to his yoke. It's a heavy yoke, but he doesn't want you to notice that. It's rough and splintery, but somehow he manages to divert your attention to something else.

So you buy the yoke. He was such a good salesman, he has you convinced that you got the best deal in Palestine. You take it in the house and your wife says, "Benny, tell me. . . . What's this? Another yoke? Benny, that's the third yoke you've bought from that guy and none of them work right!"

But you don't want to admit you've been taken, so you defend Irving. "Look Dear," you tell your wife, "Irving knows lots about yokes, and he says it's a good deal. Could you just take it easy?"

The next morning you walk out to the field, dragging this yoke behind you. You say to yourself, *I wonder about this Irving guy.* Your worst fears are confirmed when your oxen look at one another with the sort of here-we-go-again expression that only an intelligent ox could possibly muster. With some difficulty you finally get their necks in the yoke when, right on cue, both of them sit down.

Honest Irving has struck again.

Yoke of Slavery, Yoke of Love

The Bible has some interesting things to say about yokes. Slavery is called a yoke (1 Timothy 6:1). But the word is also used in a spiritual sense.

For example, Paul talked about a "yoke of slavery." But he used that as a description of legalism—trying to live the Christian life by keeping a long list of rules. He said, "It was for freedom that Christ set us free; therefore keep standing firm and do not be subject again to a yoke of slavery" (Galatians 5:1).

In other words, don't go back to Old Testament laws and the extras the Jews added to them. The Law was fulfilled in Christ.

It is interesting then to note that Jesus said that coming to Him means taking *His* yoke. But there is a sharp contrast. Christ's yoke is easy; His burden is light. He invites *tired* people to take His yoke (11:28-30).

Perhaps He wants us to think that following Him is something personal, something we share together with Him. We wear a yoke, but we are yoked together with Jesus. That's an easy yoke, a light burden.

Trying to live by a list of legal restrictions is like putting on a heavy yoke, a hard burden, going it alone. But life, Jesus-style, is teamwork with the Creator in a yoke of joy. He fulfilled the law and its demands.

The Law, the Prophets—Abolish, Fulfill?

Look at the Sermon; this time Matthew 5:17-20. Here's the good-yoke/bad-yoke theme again.

"Do not think that I came to abolish the Law or the Prophets." The Jews spoke of the entire Old Testament as "The Law and the Prophets." Jesus is saying that He is speaking with authority, but He is not contradicting the Old Testament.

"I did not come to abolish, but to fulfill" (5:17). Christ's mission was constructive. It was built on the Old Testament, a fulfillment of everything the Old Testament pointed to. Not only was Jesus the fulfillment of Old Testament predictions about a coming King—He is also the only man who ever fulfilled the demands of the Law.

"For truly I say to you, until heaven and earth pass away, not the smallest letter or stroke shall pass away from the Law, until all is accomplished" (5:18). Here is where the jot and tittle come into the picture. Those Hebrew jots and tittles are like our dots, periods, commas, and crossing of ts. Jesus did not take the written

Word of God lightly. It would *all* be fulfilled. *Someday,* Christ may have thought as He spoke, *you will see how the Cross fits into this. It will be the fulfillment of all the Old Testament sacrifices.*

"Whoever then annuls one of the least of these commandments, and so teaches others, shall be called least in the kingdom of heaven; but whoever keeps and teaches them, he shall be called great in the kingdom of heaven"(5:19).

There are different ways to "annul" God's principles. Some people eliminate His teachings by not taking the time to discover what He says.

Some people fail to fulfill God's laws by willful rejection of the Lord's message, a defiant rebellion.

Other people muddle what the Word says by adding their traditions and ideas to it. Jesus told the religious leaders that they broke God's laws by adding their own traditions to them (15:3).

We often do the same. We become more biblical than the Bible, proud of what we don't do, but never really getting around to what we *should* do.

I also note that there is a tremendous responsibility that goes along with communicating God's principles. If we add to them, change them, neglect them, or reject them, and lead others astray, we will be held accountable.

Here comes the clincher: "For I say to you, that unless your righteousness surpasses that of the scribes and Pharisees, you shall not enter the kingdom of heaven" (5:20). Our goodness should be motivated by a deep inner righteousness.

The average Jew looked up to his religious leaders quite a bit more than most Christians look up to their pastor or youth director. For Jesus to say, "You have to be better than your religious leaders" would be a discouragement. After all, who could be better than a religious leader?

But then, the whole point of the Sermon on the Mount is to show us our inability to do good. That's why the person who is poor in spirit is blessed; *he* recognizes his need. It is that person who, in his hunger and thirst for righteousness, finds life, Jesus-style.

When the Sparks Fly the Stars Still Shine

Two thousand years after the Sermon on the Mount, on a mountain in the High Sierras, I sat reading Matthew's Gospel by a flickering campfire. Occasionally the wood crackled and dozens of sparks flew upward and disappeared in the black sky. That graphically expressed my feelings. Every time I sensed a spark of success, it just swirled into the darkness and disappeared.

I had come home from my first church camp experience determined to clean up my language, and I had a spark of spiritual success. But one day, about a week after church camp, my temper flared and that spark of success crackled and swirled into the darkness.

But, since my camp commitment worked for a week, I figured I'd better start planning for the next summer. Maybe next year it'd work for a month!

The next summer came and went. Another pinecone singed. Another promise to God broken. Another spark. And darkness.

I suppose that's why I was so impressed by Matthew's Gospel that night when I was reading it with my brother. We read Matthew's account of the King's crucifixion and resurrection and, for some reason, I saw things differently. I realized for the first time that my darkness did not need my small sparks of success to illuminate it. That darkness was already stabbed by thousands of God's own stars. And each star represents a different facet of the righteousness of Jesus Christ.

For the first time in my life I was beginning to understand that *His* righteousness became mine through faith (2 Corinthians 5:21). That is the beginning point of life, Jesus-style.

3

Showdown on Anger

Some of the most vivid memories I have are memories of anger. A footstool thrown across a living room, shattered. A fistfight between a father and his son. A baseball bat flung across a highway so it wouldn't be available in the heat of an argument. A teenager nearly run over while trying to convince a friend to calm down. Two brothers bruised, one bleeding—all over a stupid disagreement.

While in high school I had a close friend with an electric temper. Jerry had a fight with his girl friend one day. That same afternoon, in a fit of rage and self-pity, he drove to Downey, California, and volunteered for the draft. Then, he was so rattled by what he had done, he backed his car into the side of the building while leaving the parking lot.

The following Sunday evening the entire youth group sat together in the back row of the church. The congregation was singing "Who Is on the Lord's Side?" When we got to the last verse, half-way through, we hit the part that goes, "Joyfully enlisting by Thy grace divine." We all looked at Jerry. He laughed. He was over his anger.

31

But the results of anger are often far-reaching. Within a month, Jerry was inducted into the army.

Showdown by Sundown

Anger is like a wild West shoot-out.

Sometimes we are ambushed by it. Wrath does its destructive work on our spirits almost before we know we're getting mad. We simply erupt. We shoot off our mouths, or whatever we do when we lose our tempers. Suddenly we feel a bit dumb and wish there was a cactus to hide behind.

But usually anger comes in the showdown variety. Like the old westerns with the deputy and the meanest hombre on the plains pacing toward one another on the dirt streets of Tombstone, we see anger coming. It's just a question of who's quickest on the draw. Will our temper get the best of us, shooting our good intentions full of holes? Or are we quick enough in spirit to handle anger God's way?

Take Ephesians 4:26-27 for example. Paul said, "Do not let the sun go down on your anger." There should be a showdown by sundown.

Now Paul didn't mean we can be "angry as sin" as long as the sun is shining, just so we cool off at dusk (or on very overcast days). No, Paul stressed the need to control our tempers. All the time.

There is a very good reason why he reminded us to control this emotion: Uncontrolled anger gives the devil a perfect opportunity (Ephesians 4:27). And he tries not to miss perfect opportunities.

Outdraw Anger, Take Careful Aim

Sometimes we have difficulty controlling our tempers because we've never taken the time to understand them. We attempt to outdraw anger without taking careful aim.

It helps to take an honest look at ourselves. Some of us have a bigger problem with anger than others, but we all need to do some self-examination.

However, we need to look deep enough to see *why* we get angry, not just what we get angry at, or what circumstances make us angry. What is at the root of it?

When we strip away all the excuses and dust off all the circumstances, we discover that uncontrolled anger is really nothing more than *selfishness expressing itself.*

We're ticked when someone cheats us. We lose control when we are nagged. We scream when someone monopolizes the TV.

Anger beats us to the draw. Our selfishness bushwhacks us. True, the other person may be wrong too, but we are responsible for the way we handle the showdown. It's part of life, Jesus-style. We have to be honest enough to face anger for exactly what it is: It's not just the way we are; it's sin.

High Standards, Strong Words

Left on our own, we cover ourselves brilliantly. Instead of "sin," anger becomes "part of our temperament," "the way we are." It's good to understand the excuses we give ourselves, because that is precisely what the Jews were doing in Jesus' day, and that is why the subject of anger wiggled its way into the Sermon.

Several years ago I went through the fifth chapter of Matthew's Gospel and did some underlining. I noticed that Jesus made some contrasts between the Jews' religious standards and His own standards (5:21-48). He had just said that His followers' righteousness had to *exceed* the righteousness of the religious leaders (5:20).

Now I'm looking at that same Bible that I had underlined and I immediately see the following contrasts:

They outlawed *murder;* He outlawed *anger* (5:21-26).

They outlawed *adultery;* He outlawed *lust* (5:27-30).

They made divorce *easy;* He *ruled it out* (5:31-32).

They called for *honest vows;* He called for *honest speech* (5:33-37).

They spoke of *retaliation;* He spoke of *self-denial* (5:38-42).

They spoke of *hate;* He spoke of *love* (5:43-48).

In each case, Jesus referred to the commonly accepted practice, the religious viewpoint. Then He presented a new standard: life, Jesus-style. His principles ran counter to the common practices of His day. I believe they also run counter to the common practices of our own day—even among Christians.

Anger: Low Road, High Road

What the Sermon says about anger is a good illustration of this (5:21-26). Would we put murder and anger in the same class? The Jews didn't. Jesus did. The Jews said, if you commit murder you are guilty before the court (5:21). Jesus said, *if you are angry with your brother* you are in danger of the court (5:22).

A little understanding of the Jewish legal system helps out a lot at this point. The Jewish leaders did a little addition and came up with their own answer. It worked like this:

> God prohibited murder (Exodus 20:13; Deuteronomy 5:17).
> + God told Israel to establish courts (Deuteronomy 16:18).
> + Israel did establish courts (2 Chronicles 19:5-6).
> = If someone commits murder, they answer to the court (Matthew 5:21).

So they established a lower court to care for minor violations. If a man was found guilty, he was in danger of judgment by that lower court.

More serious matters were handled by a supreme court, called the Sanhedrin. If this supreme court found a man guilty of some major crime they had the authority to put him to death, in which case his body was taken to the valley of Hinnom.

It was at this small valley outside Jerusalem that the city's garbage was disposed of, set on fire for complete destruction. This rubbish heap was called *Gehenna,* "the hell of fire."

With that historical information in mind, look again at the Sermon:

"Everyone who is angry with his brother," Jesus said, "shall be guilty before the court" (5:22). Those Jews would hear the word "court" and immediately think of their lower court. *That means I am in legal trouble just for being angry!*

"Whoever shall say to his brother, 'Raca,' shall be guilty before the supreme court" (5:22). *Raca* was a term of contempt. When in anger, if you look down on another person, treating him like dirt, you have said in effect, "Raca." Jesus called this a major offense.

He continued, "Whoever shall say, 'You fool,' shall be guilty enough to go into the hell of fire" (5:22). His listeners hearing the word, *Gehenna*—"hell of fire"—would immediately associate it with that specific place just outside Jerusalem in the valley of Hinnom that burned constantly. Throughout Jesus' ministry He referred to Gehenna, the hell of fire, and applied it to a future place of far greater torment, for eternity.

What's Jesus saying to us? We cannot take anger lightly. If a person never did anything else wrong, but could not control his temper, he would be worthy of hell.

Strong words.

A high standard.

Life, Jesus-style.

Brands of Anger, Degrees of Sin

We should also note the three degrees of anger in Matthew 5:22.

There is that *quiet, slow-burn anger*—suppressed; held in. Kids sometimes feel this way toward their parents—a quiet inward resentment. It's like fuming at a traffic cop who gives you a ticket. You're afraid to say anything; it might get more costly.

Some of us are proud of our ability to "control our temper," when in reality we have not controlled it; we have only suppressed it. That's not the way to handle anger. Bitterness does not evaporate just because it is ignored.

The second brand of anger Jesus refers to is *contempt*—either saying or acting out a "raca" attitude. That's when you look at the other person as if he has no value or as if he is beneath you.

Anger, brand three, is *violence* expressed by strong, nasty language. "Fool!" sounds innocent enough. We use the word rather loosely today. Jesus wasn't specifically condemning our casual use of the word, though our jokes often do deep damage to a person's self-worth. What Jesus did *specifically* condemn is the violent attitude of anger, especially when expressed with words that slash out at another person—whether "fool" is included in the vocal outburst or not.

You Can't Tame Your Tongue with a Whip and Chair

With his feet elevated, Harold sits on the tired-looking recliner reading *Popular Mechanics*. Above him on the pine paneled wall a tapestry hangs, framing him in a confused patchwork of color.

Martha, his wife of 23 years, slouches across the couch working on a needlepoint project while reading her Bible.

The kids, 16-year-old Jeff and his 11-year-old sister, argue over the precise identity of some singer.

Bernard, the family's beagle, barks at a semi that passes boisterously on a nearby highway.

At the opposite end of the room the TV speaks into the chaos.

"Would you turn that dumb thing down!" Martha shouts crossly, motioning toward the TV.

"Boy, aren't you the Christian," Jeff taunts, referring to her crabbiness.

Elisa, his sister, lets out a reprimanding, "Jeff!"

Harold turns over 50 pages in his magazine looking for the continuation of his article.

"You and your foul mouth," Martha's voice be-

You CAN'T TAME YOUR TONGUE
    WITH A WHIP AND A CHAIR —

SOMETIMES CHOMPING DOWN WITH
    YOUR TEETH HELPS!

gins to rise as she puts down her needlepoint and lifts her black Bible. And then, abruptly changing her thought, she turns toward her husband. "Harold! Do something with your boy!"

"Well, dear," he says, lowering his magazine, "he does have a point. You have got to be the most unpleasant person we talk with all week."

The incident ends with a shower of tears from the mother and long, deliberate sighs from the father and children. Another evening with the family is finished. But the damage caused by such undisciplined use of the tongue and unchecked tempers continues for a long, long time.

We can't tame our tongues with a whip and chair.

Sometimes chomping down with our teeth helps.

But the internal problem is deeper—anger, contempt, violence.

Making It Right

Back to the Sermon (5:23-26):

What if you are on your way to church or just beginning to pray when you remember there is an anger problem brewing in your life?

Jesus gave this example: A person is at the altar presenting his offering to God when *he remembers* that a brother has something against him. Rather than putting the other guy down, rather than letting it stir up quiet anger, "raca" anger, or violent anger, *he takes the initiative* to go to his brother and tries to clear things up between them.

He leaves his offering, interrupting his religious duties. He does not take advantage of a situation which would seem to offer a good excuse to procrastinate. Once the situation is resolved, *he re-turns* to give his offering to God.

Do you know anyone who would leave a church service or youth meeting to make something right with his parents, or a friend? Would you? Right now I can't help thinking about a family that is terribly fragmented, filled with the problems of quiet anger, and anger that's not so quiet. In the midst of that turmoil of tempers there is a great deal of Bible reading and prayer flaunted before the one unsaved member of the family. The damage to his life may be irreparable, humanly speaking. Why not do the Bible reading and prayer in private, while openly working to mend the rifts in the family? (Matthew 6:1-18)

Leave your gift at the altar! First, make things right with anyone who has something against you. This point is underscored in verses 25-26 as Jesus returns to the imagery of the Jewish legal system to show the importance of clearing all debts and offenses as quickly as possible.

A Postscript on Handling Anger

Yes, anger is very much like a wild West shoot-out—playing for keeps. But once you determine to handle it God's way, where do you begin?

Good question. Here are some 1-2-3 style answers for each of us to consider:

(1) Know what should make you angry, and what shouldn't. "Be angry, and yet do not sin" (Ephesians 4:26). Paul said it; Jesus demonstrated it. Remember when He cleansed the temple? He did it twice: once at the beginning of His ministry, once at the end (John 2:13-22; Matthew 21:12-13). Jesus was angry at sin when He cleansed the temple, but not on the cross.

Cleansing the temple, Jesus expressed anger and judgment.

Dying on the cross, Jesus expressed love and forgiveness.

Jesus knew what should make Him angry, and what shouldn't. His anger was *never* selfishness expressing itself. It was righteousness in action, enthusiasm for God's glory.

(2) Figure out ahead of time what makes you angry. If you are inclined toward selfishness expressing itself, a temper easily ignited, it helps to do a little spiritual target practicing.

Learn how to handle those touchy situations *before* you encounter them. You may struggle with problems over and over again that would be easier to handle if you would only work on solving them before you're uncontrollably involved in the heat of an argument.

A teen whose parents are always riding him about something (a messy room, late dates, whatever) probably finds anger a constant battle. Determining ahead of time to handle the situation in a Christian way may involve cleaning the room, or coming home earlier. When you wait till another argument flares, you almost always get burnt.

(3) When possible, avoid situations that make you angry. You can't always do that, but when you can everyone will be glad if you do.

(4) Realize that many irritations with other people arise simply because your personalities are different. The differences cause friction. She's bubbly and outgoing at 8:00 A.M. and you're still sleepy. That irks you. Well, allow room for people to be different. Next time you're tempted to write somebody off just because he's different, say a

quick prayer. Thank God that the person *isn't* just like you.

Don't try to change the world to fit your temperament. Work with the Holy Spirit in the changes He wants to make in you. Check your outlook on people and things that make you angry. This goes beyond your personality. It includes your level of spiritual maturity. Can you accept other people—faults, freaky habits, and all? Remember, God accepted you on your level of maturity—zilch by His standards.

(5) Accept situations within the framework of God's power. If God is the only One who could possibly change an irritating situation and He decides not to change it, take the hint! He wants to use it to develop your character. Don't get mad at God.

(6) Don't deny that you are angry. Once it hits, own up to it. Admit it to yourself. Admit it to God. Ask for His help.

(7) Don't lash out. This one's hard. The natural inclination is to shout first and ask questions later. As mentioned earlier, bite your tongue. Lip too, if necessary!

(8) Take your time responding to situations that irritate you. If you feel the temperature rising, slow down. Think through your response. What would Jesus do in a similar situation?

(9) Confront the other person only when confrontation is holy, righteous, and appropriate. Check out Galatians 6:1 and Matthew 18:15-20 for some pointers.

God says there is wisdom in a soft answer (Proverbs 15:1).

There is, however, a place for a "loud answer" too (see number 1). Jesus spoke calmly when He

stilled the storm (Mark 4:36-39). But I don't think
He whispered, "Please leave," when He threw the
merchants out of the temple (John 2:12-22). And
the prophets sometimes turned up their voice box
volume when they made pronouncements against
wickedness and sin.

"A gentle answer turns away wrath, but a
harsh word stirs up anger" (Proverbs 15:1).

When Jesus knew a situation called for harsh
words, He was prepared for the consequences:
Anger was stirred up in others. Unfortunately we
are not generally riled out of godly concern. Jesus
was. He shouted against sin. We whimper when
we are offended. Our selfishness expresses itself.
There is a big difference.

*(10) You can't conquer anger by merely decid-
ing to stop being angry.* You must deal with the
deeper problem: selfishness expressing itself.

That's why it doesn't work to suppress it. Trying
to hold it all inside doesn't deal with the deeper
problem. It's like pushing an inner tube to the
bottom of a pool. Much effort is required to get it
there, and even after you do it's bound to pop up
somewhere, sometime.

There are not a lot of different cures for selfishness. It's wise advice to keep in mind who's in
charge of your life. If your time, your property,
your health, and your comfort all belong to God,
what's left to get upset about?

If someone interrupts your favorite TV time,
remind yourself that it's God's time. Would He
get mad?

If someone rips off your 8-track or your CB, or
both, remember they're God's first. He knows how
to take care of what's really valuable.

If someone smashes your face, you may want to

remind the Lord that your body is the temple of His Spirit. But He didn't forget.

Anger is a tough match. But with a lot of help from the Holy Spirit, a holster filled with the Word of God, and a willing mind, you are well-equipped to handle anger God's way.

Don't let the sun go down on your anger.

4

Sex That Sours, Sex That Soars

I suppose I was about 13 when I sat in a stuffy overcrowded youth room to hear a special youth speaker. He talked about sex.

Everybody laughed at his jokes. But as he started talking seriously about sex, the room got all quiet and the temperature rose noticeably.

And as liberated as people are supposed to be today, there doesn't seem to be a great change in the reaction. The room still gets quiet and the temperature soars even if we know the lecture better than the speaker does.

I used to wonder why youth speakers sometimes seem overly preoccupied with sex. I have concluded that one of the reasons is that people—not just teens—are quickest to forget their values when it comes to sex.

Example: David
I am reminded of King David, strolling atop his palace roof, scanning the countryside with his high-powered, wide-angle binoculars. And what to his wandering eyes should appear?

Bathsheba! Taking her bath.

And, as if looking was not bad enough, David sent for the girl, "lay" with her, and got her pregnant. The problem was intensified by the fact that Bathsheba was the wife of Uriah the Hittite, one of David's generals who was out of town fighting one of David's battles.

The Plot Thickens, as They Say

David's creative solution to his dilemma was to send for Uriah and suggest that he enjoy a second honeymoon with his dear wife. After all, things must be tough out on the front lines of the old battlefield.

And things *were* tough out on the front lines. So much so that Uriah would feel guilty enjoying the good life with his wife. So instead he slept on the front steps of the royal palace.

David, in panic, activated "Plan B." He sent Uriah back to the front lines with an order that everybody else pull back, leaving Uriah all by his lonesome self, except for the enemy.

And things *were* tough out on the front lines of the battlefield—Uriah was killed.

And David married Bathsheba.

David's problem began with a look—then from look to lust, lust to adultery, adultery to murder. And some of us would have done some of the same things if we had the clout that king had.

David ultimately found his way to forgiveness. But the road back was long and uphill. (Check out the whole story in 2 Samuel 11—12).

In My Head, In My Bed . . . Why Fight It?

In the Sermon on the Mount, Jesus cuts through the underbrush and goes directly to the point. He stated the Law as the Jews understood it: "You shall not commit adultery" (Matthew 5:27). But Jesus went deeper, "But I say to you. . . " (5:28).

And what does He say? It all starts with a look. If you don't look-to-lust, you probably won't sin. If you do look-to-lust, you already have.

"Everyone," Jesus says, "who looks on a woman to lust for her has committed adultery with her already in his heart" (5:28).

Had David heard that while strolling on his roof, he may have said to himself, *Hmm, I've already done it in my head, I might as well do it in my bed.* Haven't you heard people say pretty much the same thing?

"If *thinking* it is as bad as *doing* it, why fight it?"

Answer: (1) If you *think* it and *do* it you've done it twice. (2) Thinking it does tremendous spiritual damage to you; doing it adds to that by hurting others as well. (3) You can't conquer sin by digging deeper into it.

No Bad Thoughts, No Bad Acts

There is an interesting parallel between Matthew 5:21-26 and Matthew 5:27-32. Jesus says if you have no anger, there will be no murder (5:21-26). He also says if you have no lust, there will be no adultery—no sex sin (5:27-32). He doesn't waste words. No evil thoughts = no evil acts.

I attended a seminar several years ago that put much of this into perspective. "There are three battlefields," we were told. "There is a battlefield of *thoughts,* and if you lose that battle, a battlefield of *actions,* and if you lose that battle, a battlefield of *habits.*" Moral purity becomes a question of how many battlefields you have.

The Jews outlawed *actions:* No adultery! Jesus

reminds us, Think seven!—the seventh of the Ten Commandments, no adultery—but He goes beyond that: No wrong thoughts!

I am thinking of that phrase, "look on a woman to lust for her" (5:28). And it occurs to me that this is our national sport, our national pastime. It should not surprise us that some girls resent being thought of as merchandise, appreciated only as bodies. Other girls obviously enjoy it. This command is for them also—No lust!

Solution: Radical Surgery

My blind friends assure me that it is not only "the sighted" who have a challenge living these no-look-to-lust principles. Nor is the problem solved by building a monastery on the slopes of the Himalayan foothills, away from TV, billboards, movies, and magazines. The problem is deeper. In the heart.

Sometimes it's too dark to see.

Or there's nothing to look at.

But the lust problem doesn't evaporate.

Jesus went on to share some alarming advice which, on some occasions, has been taken far more literally than originally intended.

"And if your right eye makes you stumble, tear it out, and throw it from you; for it is better for you that one of the parts of your body perish, than for your whole body to be thrown into hell" (5:29).

And He says the same of "your right hand" (5:30).

"If your right eye, or your right hand, *makes you stumble,*" suggests that we should be aware of the thing that triggers a trap. If your eyes or your hands spring your sexual snare, pluck them out; cut them off.

Note that it is your *right* eye, your *right* hand. Obviously the right hand is most valuable to right-handers. Or it is more likely to become a snare *because* you are right-handed.

Lefties can cut off a left.

But since Jesus also mentions the right *eye,* it is more likely that He is referring to the common concept that the right was somehow more valuable. This suggests a powerful point: Be willing to lose what is most valuable to you if it will help your spiritual development.

Be willing to make whatever sacrifices are necessary—regardless of cost—to avoid spiritual destruction. That might cost a friendship, or a closer relationship. But David, for instance, would have been better off blind than sinful. The same is true of us.

Know When to Stand and When to Run

I'm thinking of Joseph (Genesis 39). He had been bought by Potiphar, an Egyptian officer, but was promoted from slave to boss.

But Potiphar's wife looked-to-lust at Joseph as he minded his own official business. And when she could not persuade him with a sexy invitation, she grabbed his suit coat, fraternity jacket, or whatever it was, and invited him again," Come and lie with me."

And I imagine Joseph thought to himself, *She's too nice-looking to take time deciding what to do. I told her I'm not interested—now's the time to run.* In the process, she ripped off his coat which she later presented to her husband, Potiphar, saying, "Joseph the Jew tried to rape me!"

So Joseph wound up in prison. When he chose to run, he chose something with a price attached to it. He passed up an "enjoyable experience." And it seems to me that it was as if he plucked out his eyes and cut off his hands. He denied himself, said no to lust, and gave a powerful example for us.

Joseph knew that there comes a point where you stop "witnessing." When you're being seduced and bodily dragged toward the bedroom—or back seat—it's time to run.

Paul agreed. His advice was, "Flee from youthful lusts, and pursue after righteousness, faith, love, and peace, with those who call on the Lord from a pure heart" (2 Timothy 2:22). Peter said much the same (see 1 Peter 2:11).

It works out like this:

Sexual response is a beautiful part of the package deal called "Normal God-Created Bodies." If some attractive thing grabs you, making the kind of suggestions Potiphar's wife made, it's not really normal to be comatose. It *is* normal to be aroused. That's why the wise advice is: *Run! Pluck out your eyes! Cut off your hands!*

Paul expressed the same pluck-and-cut principle: "Consider the members of your earthly body as dead to immorality, impurity, passion, evil desire, and greed, which amounts to idolatry" (Colossians 3:5).

It's like the living sacrifice illustration of Romans 12:1. You present, or yield, your body to God as an expression of worship. You dedicate your entire body—every individual part—to be used for righteousness, rather than sin (Romans 6:11-13).

We all know Jesus' standard is high. But that's consistent with the Sermon. He is constantly pointing us toward a higher goal—life, Jesus-style.

Solo Sex

I'd like to say a word or two about masturbation because there are some people who, it seems to me, are lowering Jesus' high, no-lust standard. Saying that solo sex is the God-designed pressure-release valve to help keep your morals purring in a sex-charged culture is a cop-out. It's virtually impossible to masturbate without sex-related thoughts.

Sex-related thoughts and sexual stimulation—solo, or otherwise—*do* go together. God intended them to. He did not make the physical elements to operate independently of the mental and emotional—or the spiritual.

That's one reason for God's establishment of marriage as the perfect environment for sexual fulfillment. In the meantime—and for some people "the meantime" is quite long—no lust is the principle. No matter what it costs.

Your right eye.

Your right hand.

Sex that Sours, Sex that Soars

Number seven of the Ten Commandments—do not commit sex sin—is not some divine rip-off of the good life. God has a higher sexual relationship reserved for people who love Him enough to discipline themselves—who live life, Jesus-style.

That higher sexual relationship is the complete union of two people, coming together spiritually, emotionally, and physically. It is a total commitment to the Lord and to each other. In that atmosphere sex takes off! It soars!

When sex is cheapened from this life commitment of two people to a relationship built only on a zowie physical attraction, it should not surprise us that it sours. It ceases to be God's great gift and degenerates to fun and games for a time, spiraling down into a hellish, broken relationship.

It sours.

Speaking of Broken Relationships

Unfortunately, marriage—even "Christian" marriage—does not always soar. Far too often it sours also. When it does, a lot of people get hurt. Jesus talks about it in the Sermon.

"And it was said, 'Whoever divorces his wife, let him give her a certificate of dismissal; but I say to you that everyone who divorces his wife, except for the cause of unchastity, makes her commit adultery; and whoever marries a divorced woman commits adultery" (Matthew 5:31-32).

Here's the contrast again between what the Jews taught and life, Jesus-style.

Many of the Jews were teaching easy divorce. That's why the question of divorce came up repeatedly in Jesus' ministry. And whenever He explained His standard, people were astonished by it. They thought, *if there's no escape clause in the marriage agreement, it'd be better to stick with the single life* (Matthew 19:1-12).

Jesus refers to Moses, who in Old Testament times permitted divorce because of the hardness of the Jews' hearts. That used to bother me. Why couldn't Moses agree with Jesus? And that same question is raised in Matthew 19:7.

But Moses was *not* making divorce easier. He was trying to slow things down and protect wives who were tossed out of the house without warning because their husbands had bad days at the office.

Moses was saying in effect, "If you are going to be so sinful as to even consider divorce, at least give the girl a certificate of dismissal." There was an advantage to adding a little governmental red tape.

Jesus elevated the standard (Matthew 5:32). A certificate of divorce is not adequate. With one possible exception, even a "legal" divorce is not recognized by the Lord. The two are still one. That's why a remarriage equals unchastity, adultery.

But even that one possible exception does not mean God's blessing on a divorce. Matthew 5:32 was not given as a universal escape clause for a sour marriage.

God doesn't condemn a person for hanging in there in a difficult situation for Jesus' sake. On the other hand, the person initiating the divorce runs the risk of condemnation for not doing everything possible to preserve the marriage.

And yet, looking at that one exception just a bit differently, doesn't it emphasize the point Jesus is making in Matthew 5:27-30? The only exception mentioned is adultery—sex sin. Purity is a big priority with God.

A Postscript on Handling Lust

Let's back up to the basics: What does God say about your bod?

When it comes to bodies, God makes 'em good. Isn't that the point of Genesis 1:26-31? And isn't the whole one-flesh concept important to God? The "very good" of creation (Genesis 1:31) includes what one writer calls the "magnet principle." Sexually speaking, opposites attract. (Do they ever!)

It goes without saying that even God's best gifts can be misused. Our sex drive is an excellent example. It is too easy to wind up in the position of taking orders from our body. Before long, sex dictates. We listen, look, lust, and do.

That being the case, it's good advice to:

(1) Present your body to God as a living sacrifice (Romans 12:1). We talked about this before. Though Paul is using the word "body" to convey "all of life," it is excellent to visualize *every* part of your body as dedicated to God. That will not take the zing out of sex, since it was God who designed the zing in the first place. But when the temptations begin rolling in, it will help to remember that you dedicated to God every individual part of your body. *Every* part.

(2) Thank God for His limits and standards (1 Corinthians 6:18-20). They are given to guide, not frustrate. Know the Word. Understand the principles. Accept them as the standard of your life.

(3) Remember that your trials come personally crafted (1 Corinthians 10:13). God sends every trial as an opportunity for growth. It only becomes sin when we bungle it and submit to temptation. On the other hand, we know God has already provided a way of escape alongside the trial. No temptation is *too* great.

(4) Know when to run (2 Timothy 2:22). Some temptations are never conquered without getting out of the situation. That may mean breaking a friendship, quitting a job, saying "No!" (and meaning it).

(5) Don't be defeated by past failures (Philippians 3:13-14). Look up! Ask forgiveness (1 John 1:9). Keep going.

(6) Understand the concept of habits (Ephesians 4:25-32). God has created you with the

capacity to form habits. That can work to your benefit, or it can deepen your problem. It all depends on what you do with that habit capacity.

Paul did not just tell liars to stop lying. He said, "Speak truth" (Ephesians 4:25).

Thieves do not conquer kleptomania just by deciding to stop stealing. They are to replace that theft habit with the habit of working and giving to others (Ephesians 4:28).

We will fail if we attempt to defeat our sex-sin habit by merely determining not to do it again. Something positive must be put in its place. A new habit must replace the old one.

Notice the circumstances that usually cause your fall into sexual sin—whether with others or solo. Avoid those situations! Toss the books and magazines and get new reading material. Don't go to problem movies. Do something else. Something positive.

Remember the key concepts: Act fast—run. Make whatever sacrifices are necessary—the eye-hand principle. Put something positive in the place of negative habits. Give your body to God—every part of it.

Next time you hear some high-octane speaker talking about how quick we are to compromise when it comes to sex, and the room is getting quiet, and the temperature starts rising, enjoy the clean feeling of a clear conscience.

Life, Jesus-style!

5

Yea, Nay, What Do You Say?

I didn't used to think of myself as a liar and a cheat. Oh, there was the time I broke Mom's sewing machine and blamed it on my brother, that sort of thing. But even as much trouble as I got into as a kid—which, unfortunately, was a lot— when I was apprehended I usually coughed out the truth. For the most part.

I remember being cornered by my pastor, "Have you been monkeying with the mimeograph machine?"

"Yes," said I.

"Well monkey off," he told me.

Though I got nailed, it felt good to tell the truth—good inside, that is.

As a child one of the most frustrating experiences I had was being accused of pulling a knife on another grade-school student and telling him, "You'd better flee, kid!"

I recall so vividly standing on the steps of the school being grilled by the sixth-grade teacher and the principal, and telling them, "Look, every time I have been caught doing something wrong I

have admitted it. I didn't do this, honest. I swear I didn't!"

I swear I didn't.

I suppose we have all recognized times that our credibility might be helped if we could only place a bit more emphasis on our story. Instead of saying, "It's true," we say, "It's *really* true—I swear it!"

Isn't something either true or false? How can something be *really* true?

This desire to add a "really," "honest," or "I swear it," seems to be an admission that we find it hard to tell the truth. Maybe that's why our court system asks people to swear to tell the truth, the whole truth, and nothing but the truth. We *know* honesty comes hard. Perhaps we can squeeze the truth out of people if we hit them with a little pressure: "Do you *swear* that's the truth?"

And in the movies the lawyers always remind the witnesses, "You do realize you are under oath, don't you?"

Nice system.

But the problem is, most of us are sure that if someone wants to lie, no amount of swearing will make a difference. And, if someone wants to tell the truth, he doesn't need all the props; a yes or no is adequate.

Easier Vows: The Whys and Hows
The Sermon has a few words on truth and falsehood. And as usual Jesus calls for a higher standard. He says, "Unless your righteousness surpasses that of the scribes and Pharisees, you shall not enter the kingdom of heaven" (Matthew 5:20).

In the verses that follow, Jesus explains what it means to practice a righteousness which surpass-

es the righteousness of the religious leaders. It
means avoiding anger, not just murder (5:21-26).
It means avoiding lust, not just adultery (5:27-
32). It means avoiding all dishonesty, not just
"false vows" (5:33-37).

Regarding vows, the religious leaders said,
"You shall not make false vows, but shall fulfill
your vows to the Lord" (5:33). This was a reference to the third of the Ten Commandments
(Exodus 20:7). And that caution—Number Three
of the Big Ten—had led the Jews to be careful
about their vows. But they weren't nearly so
cautious about their everyday speech.

Any good Jew knew that God said, "You shall
not swear falsely by My name, so as to profane the
name of your God; I am the Lord" (Leviticus
19:12). And tucked away with Leviticus somewhere in their minds was this concept that the
Book of Numbers added:

"If a man makes a vow to the Lord, or takes an
oath to bind himself with a binding obligation, he
shall not violate his word; he shall do according to
all that proceeds out of his mouth" (30:2).

And for those who might be a bit slow, Moses
emphasized the point again: "When you make a
vow to the Lord your God, you shall not delay to
pay it, for it would be sin in you, and the Lord
your God will surely require it of you. However, if
you refrain from vowing, it would not be sin in
you. You shall be careful to perform what goes out
from your lips, just as you have voluntarily vowed
to the Lord your God, what you have promised"
(Deuteronomy 23:21-23).

Now, can you imagine Bernie and Irving argu-
ing over vows?

Bernie says, "Of course we've got to be careful if

we vow to God, but look Irving, the Law doesn't say anything about vowing to other people."

To which Irving responds, "Bernie, my good friend, I have known you for years, right?"

"Right."

"And I have tried so hard to do the right thing. You say, 'I need a loaf of bread,' I give you a loaf of bread, right?"

"Right."

"OK Bernie, now look, I ordered a pound of barley and you gave me this bag. I say to you, 'This seems a bit light. Are you sure this is a pound of barley?' And you say to me, 'Of course that is a pound of barley. You ask for barley, I give you barley. Why, I swear by the hairs of my head, honest!' Isn't that what you said, Bernie?"

"Right."

"Well, Bernie, I get the bag home and open it up, looking for my pound of barley and what do I get? A half pound of corn! Now Bernie, you promised me!"

"But Irving," Bernie responds, "I did not vow to the Lord, I vowed by my hair. Any Jew knows that's not so binding. Tell me, Irving, do you like popcorn?"

A Promise by Any Other Name Is Still a Promise

These vows, or oaths, that are referred to in the Old and the New Testaments were promises. They were solemn pledges. It was like saying, "God, You be my witness that what I am saying is true. If I cop out on honesty, if I lie, God, You judge me. You punish me."

And so they made their vows to God, and to other people. The whole procedure was not unlike our courtroom vows today, promising that what we say is true.

It's like promising God you will live for Him.

It's like wedding vows. A couple promises, "before God and these witnesses," that they will be faithful to one another till death separates them. They promise to care for the other person, that they will never even consider divorce—"till death do us part," the vows say. "What God has joined together, let not man put asunder."

So if you vow to God—call Him as your witness to a promise or statement—you are doing something most serious. If you vow before God and then lie, you have "taken His name in vain." He "will not leave him unpunished who takes His name in vain" (Exodus 20:7).

This creates a real problem for the person who wants to prop up his statements or his promises with a vow, but doesn't want to answer to the Lord for the truthfulness of the statement.

So what do you do? We have merely made vows, oaths, swearing, little more than figures of speech—"I swear on a stack of Bibles." We make our speech meaningless.

The Jews put together an elaborate system of lighter and weightier oaths. In doing this, they could select the precise oath for the exact occasion, and be as honest or dishonest as they wanted to be.

They would swear by heaven, by earth, by Jerusalem, or even by their own head! (Matthew 5:34-37) They felt more obligated to keep a vow if it had been made by heaven. If they were to swear by the hairs of their head, on the other hand, that was not so serious.

Some of their religious leaders even taught that

since heaven and earth would someday pass away, the oaths taken upon them would also pass away.

A Jew might swear by the temple that something were true, but would not swear by the gold of the temple. They figured the gold was more valuable.

Or he might swear by the altar that he would keep a promise, but hesitate to swear by the sacrifice on the altar.

For that reason they would often avoid swearing by the Lord. After all, they did not want to violate the third commandment. So they taught, "You shall not make false vows, but shall fulfill your vows to the Lord" (Matthew 5:33).

To Tell the Truth (About Lies)

Jesus gives a higher standard of honesty. He explains that the problem with making an oath by heaven is that it is the throne of God (5:34). So if you swear by heaven, you are really swearing by the Lord anyway.

He says that you have the same problem if you swear by the earth, or by Jerusalem (5:35). Earth is God's footstool; Jerusalem is the city of the great King.

He continues by saying that you can't even make an oath by your head, because you have no control over it (5:36). In spite of 20th-century dyes and bleaches, "You cannot make one hair white or black." You might cover up what's really there, but just let it grow and everyone will know.

Honesty always has a high priority in the Scriptures. These Jews had completely missed that spirit of the Law. A psalm, for instance, was written to praise the person who "swears to his own hurt, and does not change" (15:4). It is possible, David is saying in that psalm, to make a commitment that turns out to be more costly than originally anticipated. God praises the person who sticks with a commitment and honors his word even when it is difficult.

Jesus speaks of "counting the cost" of being His disciple (Luke 14:25-35). It is easy to make a spoken commitment and then not follow through with that commitment to God because it seems to cost more than originally anticipated.

Later in the Sermon, Jesus said, "Not everyone who says to Me, 'Lord, Lord,' will enter the kingdom of heaven; but he who does the will of My Father, who is in heaven" (Matthew 7:21). Saying what we mean, and meaning what we say, is a big thing with God.

Life: Sacred and Secular

The problem certain Jews were having was in trying to chop up life between the sacred (of God) and the secular (of the world). They figured it was OK to lie just so you didn't bring God's name into it. If you have to lie, lie creatively. And when you lie, swear you are telling the truth. Just don't swear by the Lord. Don't use His name in vain.

Jesus says, "Let your statement be, 'Yes, yes,' or 'No, no,' and anything beyond these is of evil" (Matthew 5:37). Our whole life is to be an expression of honesty. Our yes should mean yes. Our no should mean no. Honesty doesn't need a lot of verbal props, honest facial expressions, or a "stack of Bibles" to swear on.

"The earth is the Lord's," David said, "and all it contains, the world, and those who dwell in it" (Psalm 24:1). We can't carve up life like

Thanksgiving turkey, the sacred here, the secular there; a platter of white meat, a plate of dark.

That was the point the Jews missed. We miss the same point when we figure that successful politicians, businessmen, and used-car salesmen *have* to "say things a bit differently than they really are" in order to be successful.

It is the attitude that it's OK to lie for a "good cause" that led the whole nation to question our political system.

It is that fuzziness between truth and falsehood in business that leaves some Christians very, very confused. Others fail to get promotions because they have trouble stretching the truth with a clear conscience.

And why is it that most of us are not impressed when a used-car salesman tells us how low the mileage is, while pointing to the odometer? We look at that 1953 Chevy with only 12,000 miles on it, owned only by a retired florist in Upper Sandusky, and wonder.

But what do these words of Jesus mean for us if we are not politicians, or businessmen, and if we don't sell used cars, or we happen to be too young to fill out tax returns? Isn't this the point: that as Christians our "yes" is as binding as some sacred oath; that our entire life is to be lived as an expression of truth? Isn't that life, Jesus-style?

What difference would it make in parent-teen relationships, for instance, if "yes" meant yes and "no" meant no?

What would happen if we told our parents we'd be in by 11:00 P.M. and we *were* in by 11:00 P.M.?

And what would happen if "no" meant no with our friends? If "no" to a boyfriend or girl friend meant no?

The Roaring Lion is Lying

In thinking about truthfulness and lies, a striking thought occurs to me. Even in the Bible the Lord scarcely has the opportunity to communicate two chapters worth of truth (Genesis 1—2) before the first lie is introduced. It comes through Satan, the father of lies (John 8:44). He uses a sneaky, scaly creature as a mouthpiece (Genesis 3).

Down through the years, however, Satan has demonstrated some creativity in his falsehood, speaking his lies through religious leaders, and appearing as an angel of light (2 Corinthians 11: 14-15). One thing seems clear: He prefers half-truths to blatant lies. Because of their subtle deception, half-truths are probably far more ugly than obvious lies. People are more likely to believe falsehood garnished with truth, than an obvious lie served open-faced.

Some of Satan's biggest temptations came in the form of half-truth lies. Like the one in Genesis 3, or a similar one in Job 2, or the big one mentioned in Matthew 4.

To Eve: "If God really cared about you, He'd give you some of this groovy pomegranate (slurp). He says 'no' because one bite of this and you'll be like Him. Think He wants any competition?" Eve swallowed it! And so did Adam, seed and all!

To Job: "If God really cared for you. He wouldn't put it to you like this! How can you serve a God who kicks you when you're down?"

To Christ: "Come on, snap Your fingers and make this geologists' wonderland a countryside of fine cuisine! God sure ain't gonna do it for You!"

Satan is a roaring lion (1 Peter 5:8), and he's

seeking more than a bone of contention. Falsehood is a big part of his strategy. A part we
shouldn't share.

Lies: Black and White or Technicolor
(A Mysterious Monologue)

"Allow me to introduce myself: I am what's
known as a 'sanctified liar.' My friends just call me
'Little White.' LW for short.

"I exercise extreme caution—and no small
amount of discipline, mind you—to see that all
my lies are lilywhite (to throw another LW at
you).

"I'd stand on my head if necessary to communicate my loyalty to the truth. As far as I'm con-
cerned, it's a black-and-white issue. Yes sir, nasty
black untruths, and harmless, little white goodies
(and I use the term advisedly).

"Why just the other day Cathy Crabgrass asked
me how I liked her smelly outfit. I looked her
square in the eye and laid it on the line: 'Swell!'
says I. Little lies for Jesus' sake, that's what I
always say. Don't want the poor girl to have hurt
feelings or anything.

"Did I ever tell you, by the way, how I altered
my income tax return to get special offering
money for missions? God *richly* blessed that
endeavor.

"Or how about the time I added some neat stuff
to my testimony at the rest home so Jesus could
use it better?

"But the real winner was just this morning
when my wife and I showed the whole church how
selfless we were by selling our house and giving
all of our money to good ol' Deacon Delmer. Honest we did! You should have seen their eyes bug

out when I told 'em that was all we had in this world and we expected to see a more generous church as a result of our crystal clear testimo. . . .

"Oooo! My ticker!"

(*Clunk!*)

Don't Get Hung Up on the Christian Ropes

That roaring lion, Satan, not only *speaks* lies, he *lives* lies. It is possible for us to do the same. We can learn the Christian ropes so well that we go through our paces every Sunday morning and no one suspects that we are really inconsistent. We can even get to the point that *we* forget. We lie to ourselves. It is easier to say the truth than to live it.

I am impressed that Jesus was stalked by His critics throughout the years of His ministry. They watched Him closely, looking for faults. Yet, when they finally brought Him to trial, His enemies had to make up stories and pay witnesses to testify against Him (Mark 14:55-59). His life was lived in openness, honesty, and holiness (John 8:46). No deceit. No hypocrisy. No lies.

Jesus lived the truth He spoke. He invites us to follow His example; to pattern our life after Him; to live life, Jesus-style.

I didn't used to think of myself as being a liar and a cheat. I know now I was just using the wrong standard.

6

Hula Hoop Halos and Solid Steel Saints

I have this image, I just can't get it out of my mind. There's this guy in a suit, sitting on the very first pew in an attractive, formal church and looking very, very religious. The sunlight shining through the stained glass window paints his face religious-looking tones of light. And hovering over his head, like some outrageously futuristic UFO, is this enormous, pure-plastic hula-hoop halo.

Very religious.

And he's singing!

If you're saved and you know it,
   clap your hands,
   stamp your feet,
   shout "Amen!"
And forget about it.

Somehow the end of the song fizzles, and he's not sure why. He stands up, grabs his pulpit-size family Bible, and walks the aisle—out the door, to his car.

Instantly he bristles. Someone has nicked his

71

rear bumper and his "Honk If You Love Jesus!" bumper sticker is bruised.

Monday morning he files suit against the custodian who bumped—lightly—his burgundy Mark IV, while parking his beige Toyota. Someone's hula hoop is slipping.

And I am reminded that real Christianity isn't constructed in cathedrals. *Real* Christianity is chiseled from formless slabs by our right responses to the trying circumstances of everyday life.

And a lawsuit for a nicked bumper and bruised bumper sticker is not a right response.

Blind Eyes and Gummy

Can you imagine living life by the principle of retaliation?

"You spill my Coke—I'll dump your Pepsi!"

Can you picture a whole nation living by the eye-for-eye, tooth-for-tooth principle? Talk about blind eyes and gummy! Half the country squints, the other half puckers.

Look deeper.

The concept of retaliation is introduced in the Sermon: "You have heard that it was said, 'An eye for an eye and a tooth for a tooth'" (Matthew 5:38). That eye-for-eye, tooth-for-tooth principle, which was taught in the Old Testament, used to bother me. I mean, how brutal!

"Eye for eye, tooth for tooth, hand for hand, foot for foot, burn for burn, wound for wound, bruise for bruise" (Exodus 21:24-25).

The laws continue: "fracture for fracture" (Leviticus 24:20) and an additional "life for life" (Deuteronomy 19:21).

But now I have taken a closer look. And I

realize that what God's law originally outlined
and what became the common practice were two
different things. In the first place, these principles
were originally given as governmental principles,
not private practices. God didn't mean, you should
stomp on your neighbor's foot if he steps on yours.

On the other hand, every nation needs laws to
govern the people. How do you settle disputes
between citizens without laws and penalties? You
can't. And in recognition of that need for justice,
God gave instructions in His law. That law included a clause on capital punishment, "life for
life."

But instead of judgment being a matter of governmental authority, it became the common practice for the people to take matters into their own
grubby little hands. Somebody pokes out an eye,
someone else insists on the honor of doing a little
poking in return.

Here comes the second important considera-
tion: Some people wouldn't settle for "justice."
They wanted "revenge." There's a great
difference.

I have to admit, I give Moses a lot more credit
now than I used to, if I may express it that way.
He spoke God's message of judgment—the eye-
for-eye concept—but there was a lot more mercy
there than I ever realized.

Moses was *not* screaming at the people, "You've
been too easy on one another! The time has come
to bash the daylights out of each other! Here's
how it works: Number one, regarding eyes. . ."

The problem in Moses' day was "head for eye,"
"face for tooth," "arm for hand," "life for foot."
Moses was stuck with leading a bloodthirsty
bunch of revenge-happy people who were getting

their values from the heathen living around
them.

Moses was saying, "You've got it all wrong!
There should be justice among God's people, but
not revenge. An eye for an eye, but nothing more.
A tooth for a tooth, but that's all." And it was the
job of the civil authorities, Jewish law enforce-
ment people, to administer justice.

By Jesus' time, those principles had once again
degenerated to cheap revenge. The worst part of it
was, the religious leaders used the Scriptures to
support their law of retaliation.

In the Sermon, Jesus steps in and calls for a
righteousness that goes beyond that of the religious leaders (Matthew 5:20); life, Jesus-style.

One Good Turn Deserves Another

"Do not resist him who is evil; but whoever slaps
you on your right cheek, turn to him the other
also" (Matthew 5:39). There it is: One good turn
deserves another.

Jesus is ruling out personal revenge. I suppose
we shouldn't press the point too far. Even Jesus
Himself protested when He was slapped on the
cheek (John 18:22-23). He used strong words to
denounce the religious leaders (Matthew 23).

It's one thing if you're the one doing the slug-
ging. At that point you'd probably like to take
Matthew 5:39 literally. But if you are on the re-
ceiving end, you probably don't feel much like
turning the other cheek. It seems so much more
rewarding to retaliate.

I had a special friend who had the opportunity
to demonstrate this principle. He used to do a lot
of "late-night shopping for auto parts" with some
friends. And, frankly, he was a rather rowdy guy.

When he became a Christian, his friends came around to test the turn-the-other-cheek principle.

When a former buddy slugged him, he took Jesus literally, and turned the other cheek. In addition to a sore body, he had the satisfaction of knowing he had followed a biblical principle when it was difficult to do so. He also had the good feeling of knowing he had demonstrated something of the love of God, another facet of life, Jesus-style.

The Great Legal Rip-Off

Problem number two: What happens when you're taken to court, and forced to give up the shirt off your back? What about the problem of the legal rip-off?

"If anyone wants to sue you, and take your shirt, let him have your coat also" (Matthew 5:40).

This is bad enough when it's between insurance companies. I remember the time my wife and I crinkled into an Olds Toronado ahead of us while we were driving on the highway.

The man driving was quite nice. He let his little kid call the police. We exchanged information and inspected the damage: very, very little—to his car. Our car, well . . .

But I was amazed at the creativity of the other guy when it came time to report the damage to our insurance companies. He was trying to get a new car from the ground up! Everything but new radio knobs!

So our insurance rates crept up a bit. But that's nothing like the plight of a poor Jew standing before the court as the judgment is pronounced, and he's told, "OK, buddy, hand over your shirt."

The Jews had become renowned for their court-

room antics. The Old Testament prophets de-
nounced their coldness in using the courts to op-
press the poor.

Farther back in Jewish history, God had placed
limitations on what could be taken as a promise of
payment when the poor borrowed from the more
affluent. "If you ever take your neighbor's cloak
as a pledge, you are to return it to him before the
sun sets, for that is his only covering; it is his
cloak for his body. What else shall he sleep in?
And it shall come about that when he cries out to
Me, I will hear him, for I am gracious" (Exodus
22:26-27).

Yet Jesus says if someone sues you for your
shirt, your inner garment or tunic, let him have
your coat, your outer robe or cloak, also.

Jesus rules out our rights to personal property.
Instead of fighting it, give up both your tunic and
your robe. And it is your robe that is most valuable. This is an important caution: Hold your possessions loosely. Don't cling tenaciously to your
stuff.

I'd Walk a Mile for a Roman

Illustration number three: What about political
pressure? How far do you go if you disagree with
the government and it makes personal demands
on you? Answer: the second mile.

"And whoever shall force you to go one mile, go
with him two" (Matthew 5:41).

It's impossible to fully appreciate what Jesus is
saying here without some background. When the
Romans ruled Palestine, it seemed logical to solve
many of their transportation problems through
"impressment into service." If a Roman soldier
wanted someone to carry his equipment, by law,

all he had to do was ask. A person was obligated to go one mile.

Simon of Cyrene was pressed into carrying the cross Jesus was crucified on (Matthew 27:32).

And even though the obligation was only for one mile, this impressment into service could prove to be quite costly to a person's business.

Jesus is ruling out our right to time and energy. If asked to go one mile, don't argue or complain, but go two. Even if you are tired.

Paul expressed a parallel concept when he said, "Let every person be in subjection to the governing authorities. For there is no authority except from God, and those which exist are established by God. Therefore he who resists authority has opposed the ordinance of God; and they who have opposed will receive condemnation upon themselves" (Romans 13:1-2).

Yet this is more than obedience to authority. Obedience to authority is the first mile. There is something about our attitude, determination, and motive that is to lead us to go the second mile.

But why? Is this just for a witnessing opportunity? Kind of like picking up hitchhikers, then nailing them by reading the Bible through, cover to cover, while you drive the second mile.

One preacher suggested that a Roman soldier *might* be impressed by the "witness" of a person going a second mile. But it is at least as likely that it would give him the opportunity for some fun and games.

It *might* work out like this: They get to the end of Mile One and the Jew looks at the Roman and says, "I'll go another." The Roman is shocked, but doesn't plan to miss a good deal. By the end of that second mile this Roman can hardly contain himself. He runs up the side of the hill for a chat with his buddies.

"Hey, see that Jew down there in the striped tunic? Go down there and ask him to go a mile with you and see what happens."

And the soldiers spend the rest of the afternoon rolling around on the dust cackling as this Jew hoofs it all over Palestine.

But really—those Romans had an awesome spiritual responsibility because they had witnessed a demonstration of the love of God.

Life, Jesus-style.

Pardon Me, Could You Spare a Few Coins?

Situation number four: How do you handle requests for help? What do you do about panhandlers?

You hear a knock on the door and answer it. You are told, "My wife and six kids are in the car. We are from Blytheville, Arkansas, and just ran out of gas. My little ones have not eaten for two days. Can you help us out a bit?"

What do we do about giving? Most people get many requests for help from people they don't know. Do you give without hesitation to everyone who asks?

"Give to him who asks of you, and do not turn away from him who wants to borrow from you" (Matthew 5:42).

One missionary, constantly bombarded by beggars in a country where begging is part of the culture, suggests, "Maybe you can't give every time. But if you never give, your heart gets hardened."

Jesus rules out our rights to our own money. He talks about both *giving* and *lending*. We are not to cling to money. We are to regard it as owned by

God, entrusted to us to be wisely and compassionately used for Him.

We are to "give to him who asks." As God has given us an example of unselfishness, we are to act unselfishly toward parents and other family members, friends, and enemies.

We are to "not turn away from him who wants to borrow." And as we lend, we are to expect nothing in return (Luke 6:35).

Impossibly Christian, Irresistably Appealing

Somehow it always seems to be the ideal thing for the *other* guy to turn the other cheek, to give his shirt and his coat, to go the second mile, or to give without expectation of return. Yet it is this impossibly Christian, irresistably appealing style of life that in a unique way shouts a message to our world:

"We've been changed by the Creator's Son!"

But it's hard to talk about how "Jesus changes lives," if your life isn't changed. You can *say* it But when you actually "turn the other cheek," you'll really be communicating!

I am thinking again of that little man, sitting in the pew with a stained-glass glow on his face, topped off with a plastic halo. It occurs to me that if *he* turned his cheek that hula-hoop halo might crack. He just doesn't have spiritual fortitude. His is a shallow Christianity that shines in the sanctuary on Sunday, but fizzles and dies in the conflicts of real life.

Life, Jesus-style, is for solid steel saints who have learned that Christianity becomes truly Christian when they can turn the other cheek, give their coat, walk that second long mile, and give without expectation of return.

7

It's About My Foot

I have survived all kinds of teachers: strict ones, permissive ones; easy to please, impossible to please; nice ones, and ones not so nice. But of all of them, one stands out in my memory.

The first time I was ever exposed to pantheism—the belief that everything *is* God—came through this teacher. "If all these microscopic particles make up objects," he said wide-eyed, "and planets make up solar systems, and solar systems make up galaxies, why can't we assume they all make up God?"

A heavy thought to throw at a class of 11-year-olds.

He led us in creative writing and creative art exercises. "Write the first thing that comes into your mind when I say the word, 'hate.'" He repeated the project with the word, "love."

That same teacher approached class discipline with an exercise in democracy. "If we were on a desert island starting a new government, what rules would we make to govern ourselves?"

He got what he wanted:
- No gum-chewing
- No talking out of turn

- Only go to the rest room with permission
- Do your homework
- Etc., etc.

How he led the class to those desired conclusions is interesting. He drew neat circles on the chalkboard as he explained, "Your freedom ends where the other guy's toe begins. We have a responsibility to one another."

Not a bad concept: Treat your neighbor lovingly.

But who is your neighbor?

Sam Goode and the Rocky Mountain Rip-Off

One Wednesday afternoon, Sam Goode, a middle-aged trucker, was pushing his rig through its paces, winding through the mountain highways of the Rockies in Colorado.

At about 3:00 P.M. a Cadillac El Dorado flashed past him on one of the few straightaways approaching a 12,000-foot peak.

Farther down the road, a gang of hoods in an olive-green panel truck ran that Cadillac off the road, totaling the car and seriously injuring the driver. Then they ripped off his wallet and the Samsonite luggage they found in the trunk. They left him slouched over the steering wheel, bleeding.

About a half hour later a preacher drove by in an old Plymouth on his way home from a spiritual retreat at a campground high in the Rockies. He saw the bashed up car and wounded businessman and glanced at his wristwatch.

If he stopped to help he wouldn't make it back to his country church in time to lead prayer meeting. No one else in the church was qualified. So he tromped on the accelerator and sped on his way.

Tonight, he thought, *I'll mention this man's need for prayer.*

About that time Sam Goode came truckin' around the bend. He saw the car, recognized it as the one that had passed him earlier, and decided he should help. Sam began down-shifting, and slowed to a stop next to the demolished El Dorado.

He climbed down from his cab, administered first aid, helped the man in his cab, and took off. As they roared down the highway, Sam called the hospital on his CB.

"I have to deliver this load of soy beans," he said. "But listen, take good care of the man. When I roll back through here next week, I'll stop and check on things.

"After all," Sam continued, grinning, "what are neighbors for?"

Love, Hate, Shut the Gate

Yes, what *are* neighbors for?

Throughout His ministry, Jesus' Jewish audience had no problem with the *words,* "Love your neighbor" (Luke 10:27). That was an Old Testament concept (Leviticus 19:18). But the Jews ran into problems finding the right definition of "neighbor."

A religious leader asked Jesus, "Teacher, what shall I do to inherit eternal life?" (Luke 10:25) Jesus answered his question with a question: "What is written in the Law?" (10:26)

In response the religious leader quoted Deuteronomy 6:5 and Leviticus 19:18, back to back. "You shall love the Lord your God with all your heart, and with all your soul, and with all your strength, and with all your mind; and your neighbor as yourself" (Luke 10:27).

Jesus commended the man for his right answer, then added, "Do this, and you will live" (10:28). I get the impression that this religious leader knew there was a deeper point in Jesus' response. I think that leader began to squirm.

He was so eager to come out looking good that he searched his mind for another question, hoping to get some new data that would clear him. "And who is my neighbor?" (10:29) It was in answer to this question that Jesus told the Good Samaritan story.

Jesus wanted this religious leader to understand that his neighbor is any person in need. You can't shut the gate on a person who is hurting just because he's not a close friend, or because he happens to have a different color skin, or different religious convictions.

But Jesus was making a higher point. He presented a higher standard. A standard that will not lead you to ask the implied question: "Whom do I *not* have to love?" A standard that will lead you to love everybody.

They Say, I Say. One More Time

This brings us to the sixth of the they-say-I-say contrasts in the Sermon on the Mount. The religious leaders said, "You shall love your neighbor, and hate your enemy" (Matthew 5:43). But Jesus is again calling for a higher standard, a righteousness that surpasses that of the religious leaders (5:20). It is not good enough to love neighbors and hate enemies. There must be love for everyone—that's life, Jesus-style.

If we really love our neighbor, there will be no enemy to hate. But first, we must know who our neighbor is.

The religious leaders had messed up the Law by the traditions they added to it.

They knew Leviticus said, "Love your neighbor," but since the Lord had commanded Israel to "clear the Promised Land," as an act of His judgment, they felt justified in adding the phrase, "and hate your enemies."

Yet, even though the Lord commanded justice, He also said in the Old Testament, "You shall not detest an Edomite, for he is your brother; you shall not detest an Egyptian, because you were an alien in his land" (Deuteronomy 23:7).

And when the Apostle Paul said, "If your enemy is hungry, feed him, and if he is thirsty, give him a drink" (Romans 12:20), he was quoting the Old Testament (Proverbs 25:21).

So, what's the other half of the they-say-I-say contrast? "Love your enemies, and pray for those who persecute you" (Matthew 5:44).

There are Old Testament examples of this type of reaction. David passed up a choice opportunity to turn King Saul into a royal shish kebab, yet Saul still pursued him.

Sometime later Saul admitted, "You are more righteous than I; for you have dealt well with me, while I have dealt wickedly with you" (1 Samuel 24:17). You'd think any good Jew would rather copy David than Saul.

Jesus loved His enemies and prayed for those persecuting Him while He was on the cross (Luke 23:34). He asked God to give His executioners good things in response to the bad things they were giving Him.

Peter tells us not to return "evil for evil, or insult for insult, but give a blessing instead" (1 Peter 3:9).

Sunshine and Rain, You Do the Same

We are to love our enemies and pray for our persecutors, to demonstrate that God is our Father.

"For He causes His sun to rise on the evil and the good, and sends rain on the righteous and the unrighteous" (Matthew 5:45).

It is God's character to give His good gifts to everyone—the good, the evil, the just, the unjust. Theologians call it "common grace." If God is our Father, we should share something of His character.

How should these verses affect our relationships with people who aren't attractive? Or who are handicapped? Or whose personalities seem to be short on zing?

And for that matter, what is Jesus saying about our relationships with brothers, sisters, parents, and children? The Jews taught that we should love our neighbors; yet many Christians are most hateful toward those who are closest to them—their parents, husband or wife, sisters, brothers.

For Sale Cheap: One Used Tax Booth

"If you love those who love you, what reward have you? Do not even the tax gatherers do the same? And if you greet your brothers only, what do you do more than others? Do not even the Gentiles do the same?" (Matthew 5:46-47).

Did you ever wonder why tax collectors were considered terrible sinners in Jesus' day? They were like parasites living off their own countrymen, living off their markup on Roman taxes.

And among Jesus' followers was a man named Levi, a former tax collector who became one of the 12 disciples. He was also called Matthew.

It was an important day on the Palestinian

hillsides when God changed Levi's life. The Israeli revenues for Rome he used to get were collected by some other rip-off artist. Matthew turned to fishing—for men.

Years later, Levi's Leader left for heaven. And He left Levi. "Write about Me," Jesus said. And Matthew began the taxing job of putting together a book about his Master, his account of the Gospel.

Jesus is still looking for people who will leave their old lives and receive the completely new lives He has for them. And one of the first things He changes is our attitude toward love and hate.

It's normal, natural, and easy to give good in return for good—"I'll trade you a pint of Bubble-Up for 16 ounces of Seven Up."

It's fine to do favors for friends; it's great to greet brothers, but what are we doing more than others? And isn't this the point of the Sermon that we are obligated to do *more*?

"For I say to you, that unless your righteousness surpasses that of the scribes and Pharisees, you shall not enter the kingdom of heaven" (Matthew 5:20).

This righteousness that surpasses that of the religious leaders, this giving without expectation of return, this kindness to everybody, love for enemies, and sincere prayer for our persecutors is what it means to live life, Jesus-style.

Therefore Be Perfect

Jesus constantly keeps His higher goal for life before us. He introduced it with the nine "blesseds" we call the Beatitudes (Matthew 5:3-11). Each of the nine characteristics He gave should cause us to question our own goodness:

Do we really hunger and thirst for righteousness? Or do we just munch on it a bit between meals of selfishness and pride?

Just how pure in heart are we? Would we want our thoughts monitored for everyone to read?

The Beatitudes, then, describe a person whose righteousness really does go way beyond that of the religious leaders of Jesus' day. That person is the salt of the earth and the light of the world, preserving the world from total decay and complete destruction (5:13-16).

And since this style of righteousness is not something we can slap together with our own effort and ingenuity, Jesus came. He came to fulfill the Law and the Prophets, not to abolish them (5:17-20). And Christ fulfilled them in His own life, in His death and resurrection, and now in those of us who trust in Him.

In order to bring our attention to our need of His righteousness, Jesus gave illustrations of righteousness in His "they-say-I-say" contrasts (5:21-47). Righteousness is an incredibly high standard—life, Jesus-style.

Instead of love for neighbors and hate for enemies, Jesus calls us to love everyone:

If there is love, there will be no problems with uncontrolled anger (5:21-26).

If love controls us, we will not be dominated by lust (5:27-30).

If love reigns, marriage will be for keeps (5:31-32).

If we are motivated by love, we will be totally honest in all relationships (5:33-37).

If we are living by the principle of God's love, we will not try to get even when wronged (5:38-42).

If we know love, hate will be crushed—even our hate for our enemies (5:43-47).

A person would have to have God as his Father to live like this. The standard is unmistakably supernatural.

So Jesus concludes this section, "Therefore you are to be perfect, as your heavenly Father is perfect" (5:48).

We are to be complete and mature in God's righteousness. This doesn't mean keeping the religious traditions others are so proud of; it means obedience to God's principles from a pure motive.

God saw our inability to live righteous lives. So instead of compromising His standards, Jesus came to fulfill the Law, the Prophets, and the Sermon, as our Representative. He died. He rose. For us.

God looked at Jesus, who was carrying all our sin, and considered Him to be sin for us, letting Him take the penalty for all our wickedness (1 Corinthians 5:21). God looks at us who are believers; He sees Jesus and His perfection. And that perfection is ours by faith. Talk about fulfilling the Law and Prophets!

This is the big transaction God made with all mankind through Jesus: our sin for His perfection and righteousness.

Once we are "in Christ," our new life begins to express itself (2 Corinthians 5:17). We are changed: new values; new attitudes; life, Jesus-style. This is a growing thing.

So in a sense we are made "perfect" the second we become Christians, and in another sense we are starting a new life of growth and change, developing and maturing toward completeness and perfection.

It's About My Foot

"My freedom ends where your toe begins." It would be far too easy for us to sort of ignore the Sermon on the Mount and tell ourselves:

God never meant for us to live like that. He just wanted to show us we need Him. Now that we are Christians we can First-John-One-Nine all our blues away and boogie right into heaven.

But still it is hard to evade Jesus' words, "Therefore you are to be perfect, as your heavenly Father is perfect."

My fifth-grade teacher was wrong about pantheism—everything is not God. And some of his ideas were a bit strange—I'm not sure what's wrong with chewing gum on a desert island. But his concept of freedom wasn't bad. It just didn't go far enough.

My freedom doesn't end where your toe begins. It ends long before I get there. Freedom ends and begins when I love my enemies, and turn my cheek, tell the truth, keep my thoughts pure, and say no to my anger.

This is a higher standard.

This is real freedom.

This is life, Jesus-style.

8

When Goodness and Pride Collide

A high school junior tearfully goes to the front of the church following an emotional service. His determined statement: "I'll go where God wants me to go. I'll do what He wants me to do." But his heart is still glued to the pew.

Everyone praises him; just what he wanted. But God wanted his heart.

Showcase Christianity . . . what is it?

Two college guys stand on the Huntington Beach pier, look out over the Pacific Ocean, and talk. They came to tell the scores of people about Christ. Both are scared, each waiting for the other to start.

One leaps into a conversation with an innocent passerby, his heart pounding with fear—and with the hope that his buddy will cheer his holiness. After all, if it's so scary to witness, he might as well get a pat on the back for his efforts.

Just what is Showcase Christianity?

A young couple highly regarded in a New Testament church sold all their property and possessions, generously giving a good share of it to the church. They said they gave it all—but they didn't.

The money probably would have bought at least six new pews. But before the engraver could finish the "generously-donated-by" plaque, the Apostle Peter changed it to: "Here Lie Ananias and Sapphira—Showcase Christians!" (Acts 5:1-11)

I can identify with the dead duo. I have the same struggle with Showcase Christianity. My goodness and pride often collide.

I wonder. What would happen if God approached people today in precisely the same way He did with Ananias and Sapphira? I suppose it would be sacrilege to suggest that maybe God would change His mind when He'd see how quickly the church would die off.

Four Verses, One Concept

We can see a marked change in the Sermon content now. And Jesus gives a warning:

"Beware of practicing your righteousness before men to be noticed by them; otherwise you have no reward with your Father who is in heaven" (Matthew 6:1).

If we glance at the preceding verse, we find the concept of perfection. "Therefore, you are to be perfect, as your heavenly Father is perfect" (5:48).

Forget the chapter break for a moment. When perfection becomes our objective (5:48), it must be balanced by humility (6:1).

Now read Matthew 6:1 with 5:20 in mind. Our righteousness must surpass that of the religious leaders (5:20), but we must beware of practicing that righteousness before people just so they can see it (6:1).

Read Matthew 6:1 in view of 5:16. We are to let our light shine before men, exposing our good works (5:16), but we are not to do that in order to be seen by men (6:1). That is never to be our motive.

We are to be the light of the world.

Our righteousness is to surpass that of the religious leaders.

We are to be perfect.

But in shining our light, practicing our righteousness, displaying our "perfection," we are never to go for glory. Our goodness must never collide with pride.

Alms and Joy

To make His point, Jesus selects three common religious practices of His day and contrasts the way the Jews observed them with life, Jesus-style. He talks about *alms*—giving offerings of money, clothing, or food; *prayer*—fellowship and communication with God; and *fasting*—not eating food so one can concentrate on the Lord.

"When therefore you give alms, do not sound a trumpet before you, as the hypocrites do in the synagogues and in the streets that they may be honored by men" (6:2).

It's easy to visualize some Pharisee with a pouch of coins in one hand and a baton in the other—maybe one of those big batons like the drum majors use when they march in parades. Can you imagine this guy directing a small brass ensemble, climaxing a trumpet fanfare with a pious amen and the clink of coins as he ceremoniously drops them on the cobblestones?

The poor folks scurry around trying to collect every cent, and think to themselves, *This fellow is really religious. He gave more than the guy who came yesterday.*

Jesus calls that man a hypocrite, and says he already has his reward in full—all now, nothing later. In his hypocrisy, he has mixed a little truth with a lot of dishonesty, and has fooled a lot of people. He may even have fooled himself. But he didn't slip anything past God.

We should help the poor, "But when you give alms, do not let your left hand know what your right hand is doing; that your alms may be in secret; and your Father who sees in secret will repay you" (6:3-4).

Secrecy is a big thing with God. He knows we're most likely to fall when we think we're standing firm (1 Corinthians 10:12). The best way to avoid the spiritual pride that will cause us to trip up is to not assume we've got it made. Let God have all the credit. Don't fold your hands; your left might tell your right!

Private Prayer or Open Eye

"When you pray, you are not to be as the hypocrites; for they love to stand and pray in the synagogues and on the street corners, in order to be seen by men. Truly I say to you, they have their reward in full" (6:5).

Note the similarities: Not only do the hypocrites stand in the synagogues and on the street corners and pass out money, but they stand there and pray! Here they are, standing on a busy street corner, people all around, in the middle of a conversation with someone. The feeling hits them: prayer time!

Zap! Just like that the conversation is ended, they assume a posture of prayer, and go at it out loud. Perhaps peeking out the corners of their eyes. Who's watching me today?

Praying in private, talking with God, didn't turn them on. If they prayed in private, who'd be there to hear? Who, indeed?

Jesus talks about His way to pray (6:6-15). And point one is *secrecy*: "But you, when you pray, go into your inner room, and when you have shut your door, pray to your Father who is in secret, and your Father who sees in secret will repay you" (6:6).

Jesus doesn't just say, "Go into your inner room." He also says, "Shut the door." And we can almost hear the Father say, "Come on, forget about other people for a few minutes and talk with *Me!*"

This doesn't mean we never pray with other people. The Bible has a lot of examples of "public prayer"—these prayers are almost always quite short.

We should pray *pointedly*: "When you are praying, do not use meaningless repetition, as the Gentiles do, for they suppose that they will be heard for their many words. Therefore do not be like them; for your Father knows what you need, before you ask Him" (6:7-8).

The Gentiles had a wrong concept of God, so it's not surprising that they had a wrong concept of prayer. Their gods were too small and far too impersonal.

So how do you get something out of a minigod? Bug the daylights out of him. Give him no rest. Wear him out. Sooner or later he will buckle and give in.

This doesn't mean that we're not to pray for the same thing more than once. In the Garden of

Gethsemane Jesus prayed three times for the same thing, using the same words (Matthew 26:44). Paul prayed three times about his thorn problem (2 Corinthians 12:8-9). And Jesus invites us, even in this Sermon, to pray persistently.

But Jesus *is* ruling out "meaningless repetition." It is an insult to God. Even the words, "meaningless repetition," suggest a person who is trying to improve that last word by repeating it with another attempt.

We are invited to pray differently. Our Father knows our needs before we ask (Matthew 6:8). And good fathers care. Our prayer then, is not for the purpose of educating God, but for the purpose of friendship and communication. And, even though He knows our needs before we ask, James says, "You do not have because you do not ask" (James 4:2). Or we ask in the wrong way (4:3). Prayer is not optional.

Thy Will Be Done on Earth as in Heaven . . . Just So It's Heavenly!

The question is inescapable: "If God knows what I need, and cares like a father, why does He treat me this way?"

We must face it. Hardship *is* a part of God's good plan for us. I think of Paul the Apostle and all he went through and I ask myself, *Where does opposition and suffering rate on my value list?*

Paul told the church at Philippi that he would much rather go to heaven and be with Christ than continue to live on earth. But he was willing and prepared to stay and help the Philippians, even though he was aware that hanging around would involve more opposition, more suffering (Philippians 1:21-26).

Would we say that?

Would we say, "Here I am Lord!"—in fine Isaiah fashion—"Crush me!"

Would we pray, "Thy will be done on earth as it is in heaven," if we knew His will for us included suffering and opposition? Anticipating Christ's presence must involve not only a passion to *see* Jesus, but a willingness to have His purposes fulfilled in us.

"Thy will be done." If His will includes suffering, hardship, and opposition, shouldn't we willingly and praisefully submit in the same way that we anticipate His return? Or the good and pleasant things He gives?

"Thy kingdom come." Maybe the reason we are not so hot on opposition and suffering is the same reason we're not truly eager to see Jesus at all. It'd spoil everything! Our hobbies. Our values. Our future plans. Our love life. Tonight's TV programs.

"Pray, then, in this way: 'Our Father who art in heaven, hallowed be Thy name. Thy kingdom come. Thy will be done, on earth as it is in heaven. Give us this day our daily bread. And forgive us our debts, as we also have forgiven our debtors. And do not lead us into temptation, but deliver us from evil. For Thine is the kingdom, and the power, and the glory, forever. Amen'" (Matthew 6:9-13).

We pray that God's name will be hallowed—set apart as holy and greatly respected. We acknowledge His holiness, but we come to Him in a Father/child relationship.

We pray about God's kingdom: that it will come. We eagerly anticipate the Lord's return and His full outward control of all things.

We pray about God's will: that it will be done. After all, that is the purpose that will be fulfilled in heaven. Christ constantly kept the Father's will in front of Him. That's why He came (Hebrews 10:7).

We pray about our daily bread: that God will provide it, day by day. We don't ask for days without suffering. God has not promised that. He invites us to simplify our lives, to be content with food enough for today.

We pray about forgiveness: that God will forgive us in the same measure that we forgive others. If we pray with vengeance or hatred in our lives, we are asking God to give us the same treatment.

We pray about temptation: that God will deliver us from it. In the middle of every testing, we look to God for His way of escape (1 Corinthians 10:13). As Jesus suggested to His disciples on the night of His arrest, we should pray that we won't enter temptation (Luke 22:40). We need His help.

Matthew cautions us, "Forgive to be forgiven" (6:14-15). As bitterness breeds bitterness, so forgiveness breeds forgiveness—and love. Of the six requests mentioned in the prayer, forgiveness is the only one that gets additional comment. Think maybe Jesus was trying to tell us something?

Trusting God for grace to forgive those who offend us is more difficult than trusting God for our daily food, or even for deliverance out of temptation.

Life, Jesus-style—His standard of righteousness—means we do not practice our righteousness to be seen by men. We do it secretly (6:1). We give without fanfare (6:2-4). We pray in private (6:5-15). We fast in secret (6:16-18).

Don't Fast Slow

"Whenever you fast, do not put on a gloomy face as the hypocrites do; for they neglect their appearance in order to be seen fasting by men. Truly I say to you, they have their reward in full" (Matthew 6:16).

These Jews evidently tried to look sick and scraggly when they fasted. Can you imagine an ashen-faced Jew in a wrinkled robe, sucking in his cheeks, and making gurgling sounds so people will think his stomach is growling? This is righteousness?

"But you," Jesus said, "when you fast, anoint your head, and wash your face; so that you may not be seen fasting by men, but by your Father who is in secret; and your Father who sees in secret will repay you" (Matthew 6:17-18).

The Jews anointed their heads on feast days, not fast days. But Jesus said, "Anoint your head, and wash your face." Do not make it your aim to be seen and admired by men. Instead cover up your act of fasting. Be joyful! Do it in secret.

Mum's the Word

Jesus draws several parallels between giving alms, praying, and fasting. In each case, mum's the word. Do it in secret. Do not draw attention to yourself. Don't blow trumpets, or clank your coins in the offering plate, or flash your bills. Don't scream your prayers in the middle of a busy intersection. Don't announce your spiritual sacrificing, fasting or otherwise.

Then too, in each case Jesus suggests the possibility of forfeiting rewards. If we do good deeds for the praise of people, their praise will be our only reward. There will be nothing from God.

On the contrary, if we live life, Jesus-style, we will be seen by our Father, who is in secret, and who sees in secret. He will repay us. He doesn't seem to "see" righteousness done for the public eye. When goodness and pride collide, He seems to look the other way.

9

Treasure on Layaway

When I was younger I thought someone had to own half the world, a third of the moon, and a McDonald's franchise before he could honestly be called wealthy.

So here I am, older and I trust wiser, asking myself the question, "How much money do you have to have before you are considered rich?"

I now answer, "It all depends . . ."

And, "How much money do you have to have before materialism or worldliness become a problem?" That all depends too. Maybe all you need is a pocket full of change and a wrong attitude.

Maybe less than that.

I Was a Teenage Materialist
By Gimmie Moore

"There's only one thing I ever wanted out of life. Just one . . . *more!*

"I remember when Hula Hoops were really in. I used to hula with six. One around my head. Two around my chest. Two around my waist. And one on my left foot. That was a wild sight!

I RECALL WHEN HULA HOOPS WERE IN...
I USED TO HULA WITH SIX!

"I quickly learned the importance of placing first things first. I was always first in line at the cafeteria in grade school. I was first in line at high school graduation. (And with a name like "Moore" you can imagine I had to do some fancy diploma tradin' after the ceremony.) I was first in line for registration my first year of college. That was a scream! I got the pick of the freebie deodorant and hair goop that advertisers give to new students.

"It occurs to me that Jesus said someplace, "The last will be least" or something like that. I make it my aim to heed that cautionary note.

"There are precious few things more important in life than Moore. Just last Sunday in church Pastor prayed and the organ played softly—it was invitation time. "Altar hour," I call it.

"I heard that organ and that sweetly familiar tune, and these words ran through my mind over and over:

> *Jesus is all the world to me—*
> *My car, my boat, my date!*
> *I'll trust Him now to keep me rich*
> *So I can buy 8-track tapes!*
> *Beautiful life with all I need,*
> *With burgers and fries my mouth He*
> *feeds!*
> *Beautiful life! Burgers and fries!*
> *He's my Friend!*

"I was the first person to walk the aisle."

Lay It Out, Stack It Up

Jesus talks about our attitudes toward wealth. And He challenges our concepts of security.

"Do not lay up for yourselves treasures upon earth, where moth and rust destroy, and where thieves break in and steal" (Matthew 6:19).

Jesus has just talked about giving alms, prayer, and fasting. His discussion about money and values follows logically.

It is not to be our habit to "lay up treasures upon earth," which in Jesus' day included such valuables as money, clothing, houses, corn, wine, and oil. There are too many destructive elements on earth. All of these things will disappear.

First, you have this problem of moths and rust. Give them a little time with your stuff and all you will have is the dust of depreciation.

And second, even if the moths pass you by and the rust is delayed, there are always thieves who will dig through those mud walls and sun-dried bricks and rip you off. Better find a higher security—a different value system.

Here's Jesus' contrast: Don't collect treasures on earth, "but lay up for yourselves treasures in heaven, where neither moth nor rust destroys, and where thieves do not break in or steal" (6:20).

Sounds a lot like the Apostle Paul: "If then you have been raised up with Christ, keep seeking the things above, where Christ is, seated at the right hand of God. Set your mind on the things above, not on the things that are on the earth. For you have died and your life is hidden with Christ in God" (Colossians 3:1-3).

Jesus says, "Where your treasure is, there will your heart be also" (Matthew 6:21). It's *possible* to be rich and Christian, but it is hard. For that reason the psalmist cautioned: "If riches increase, do not set your heart upon them" (Psalm 62:10).

Bad Eyes, Two Masters. Good Eyes, One

A wrong value system is like poor eyesight. The eyes will not focus properly, or your right eye

looks east while your left eye looks north. Whatever. A wrong set of values is like trying to keep
one eye on heaven, and the other on your wallet.
You have nothing to show for it but a stiff neck.

"The lamp of the body," Jesus says, "is the eye;
if therefore your eye is clear, your whole body will
be full of light. But if your eye is bad, your whole
body will be full of darkness. If therefore the light
that is in you is darkness, how great is the darkness!" (Matthew 6:22-23)

Paul talks about the importance of not "looking"
on the things that are seen, if you can imagine
that. Instead we are to look on the things that are
not seen. The things that are seen are temporary.
The things that are not seen are eternal (2 Corinthians 4:18). It's a different value system—life,
Jesus-style.

To state the same principle in a different way:
"No one can serve two masters; for either he will
hate the one and love the other, or he will hold to
one and despise the other. You cannot serve God
and Mammon" (Matthew 6:24).

For the person who has decided to live life,
Jesus-style, the value conflict comes when he attempts to be the bond-slave of God and of personal
wealth simultaneously. It will not work. Two
masters create an unbearable conflict of interests.
The two are not saying the same thing.

When Jesus says, "You cannot serve God and
Mammon," He does not just mean you *shouldn't*
serve both. He means you *can't* serve both.
Mammon—the money-god, devotion to riches—
screams at you, "Hoard your money; look out for
yourself; get ahead; think security!"

Jesus is not contrasting affluence with poverty.
These verses contrast two motives or attitudes

toward money. The question is resolved when Jesus becomes Lord of our finances, whether we are affluent, or whether we are poor.

Food, Drink, What Do You Think?

Jesus also talks about our attitudes toward the necessities of life. He rules out anxiety, worry.

He is still talking about our attitudes toward money, obviously.

"You cannot serve God and Mammon. For this reason I say to you, do not be anxious for your life, as to what you shall eat, or what you shall drink; nor for your body, as to what you shall put on. Is not life more than food, and the body than clothing?" (Matthew 6:25)

Notice Jesus' words, "Do not be anxious." He says the same words in verses 31 and 34. And each time He repeats, "Do not be anxious," He gives a different reason.

Do not be anxious, because it is unnecessary. Someone is already looking out for our needs. Don't worry about what to eat. Don't worry about what to drink. Don't worry about what to wear. Life is more than food. The body is more than clothing.

Jesus told Satan, "Man shall not live on bread alone, but on every word that proceeds out of the mouth of God" (Matthew 4:4).

Not only do we sometimes worry about having food enough to eat, but we also worry about eating a particular type of food.

And we say, "Do we have to have hamburgers again?" Or, "I'm tired of hot dogs!" Meanwhile on the other side of the globe, and on this side too, hundreds of people die daily from hunger. Something is wrong with our values.

Have You Ever Seen a Bird in Bib Overalls?

"Look at the birds of the air, that they do not sow, neither do they reap, nor gather into barns, and yet your heavenly Father feeds them. Are you not worth much more than they?" (Matthew 6:26)

Jesus is telling us that being anxious is unnecessary. Now He points to Exhibit A: the birds. They do not plant. They do not harvest. They do not build barns to store their food. In spite of that, God feeds them.

Jesus concludes with the question: "Are you not worth much more than they?" Implied answer: "Of course we are."

Now that doesn't mean we should get a tube of Elmer's glue and plaster our arms with chicken feathers, move out into the fields, look up into the sky with an expectant look, and chant, "What, me worry?"

We have a responsibility to be diligent. The birds do not plant, harvest, or store in barns, but God has given us brains and abilities to do just that.

"If anyone does not provide for his own, and especially for those of his household, he has denied the faith, and is worse than an unbeliever" (1 Timothy 5:8).

And "if anyone will not work, neither let him eat" (2 Thessalonians 3:10). We should assume some responsibility. But as we do, Jesus says, "Don't worry!"

A Life That's Longer, or a Cubit Taller?

Worry is unnecessary. It won't make us taller. We won't live longer. And we won't be any warmer.

"And which of you by being anxious can add a single cubit to his life's span? And why are you anxious about clothing? Observe how the lilies of the field grow; they do not toil nor do they spin, yet I say to you that even Solomon in all his glory did not clothe himself like one of these" (Matthew 6:27-29).

I can't help wondering which age-group worries more about clothing. And I'm not sure. I know some middle-aged people who could care less what they wear. I have met a few, on the other hand, who look ridiculously current.

I know many teenagers who die the death of dismay if their parents force them to wear something that's a bit out of style. And it seems that it is easy for us to have the same attitude toward clothing that we have with food.

We may not worry *if* we will eat, but we sure worry if we will be able to eat exactly what we want. We may not worry *if* we will have clothes to wear but, oh, do we ever worry if our clothes will be stylish. And "stylish" may mean anything from creased just right, to patches in the proper places.

In Jesus' day the royal look was in style and He said, "Look at the flowers and relax." But while you are relaxing, work without worry. Flowers do not toil or spin, but we had better do just that. It's one of the ways God is providing for us.

"But if God so arrays the grass of the field, which is alive today and tomorrow is thrown into the furnace, will He not much more do so for you, O men of little faith?" (Matthew 6:30)

Since trees were scarce in Palestine, the Jews gathered common grass and used it as fuel in their fires for heating and baking. If they didn't gather it, it would wither anyway. But look at the investment God made in its beauty. He cares more about us.

Don't Hide What You Seek

Jesus said, *Do not be anxious, because it is unnecessary* (6:25-30). He also says, *Do not be anxious, because it is improper* (6:31-33).

"Do not be anxious then, saying, 'What shall we eat?' or, 'What shall we drink?' or, 'With what shall we clothe ourselves?' For all these things the Gentiles eagerly seek; for your heavenly Father knows that you need all these things" (6:31-32).

Unbelievers are uptight because they do not have a Father/child relationship with God. Christians do. It should make a difference.

We see a sharp contrast: "But seek first His kingdom, and His righteousness; and all these things shall be added to you" (6:33).

People who do not know God *seek* after food, drink, clothing first. They earnestly seek security in money and possessions.

But the person who lives life, Jesus-style, is actively seeking God's righteousness. And it is that hunger and thirst for righteousness which God says He will satisfy (Matthew 5:6).

As for our necessities, Jesus says, "All these things shall be added" (6:33). He invites us to pray for our "daily bread" (6:11). But He does not guarantee freedom from hunger, need, or persecution. He tells us, no matter what our circumstances, to not worry, but to seek His kingdom and hunger for His righteousness.

Another Day, Another Trauma

Anxiety is unnecessary (6:25-30). *Anxiety is improper* (6:31-33). *Anxiety is unproductive* (6:34).

"Therefore do not be anxious for tomorrow; for tomorrow will care for itself. Each day has enough trouble of its own" (6:34).

There it is, Jesus' third command and third reason: *Do not be anxious, because it is unproductive.* You can't kill tomorrow's traumas with today's worry.

What kinds of things do we worry about? Most of our worries are about "tomorrow." And it's interesting, many of the things we tend to worry about never happen anyway. So there it is, a hunk of wasted worry.

Let's face it, though: A lot of things we do worry about *do* happen. And quite a few we don't anticipate. And Jesus tells us, "You better believe you will have adversity! In this world you will have all kinds of tribulation" (John 16:33). But take each day fresh. Trust God regardless. Seek His kingdom, and His righteousness. And someday He will reward your righteousness. His kingdom *will* come. He will wipe away your tears, and you will forget what hardship is."

How much money do you have to have before materialism or worldliness becomes a problem?

None.

But as we seek God's kingdom and God's righteousness, we see our values turn inside-out and upside-down, and we enter into life, Jesus-style.

10

My Soap, Your Laundry

I have a quaint proverb to share. It sounds like it came off a Christian fortune cookie.

Before pouring spot remover on my brother's laundry, I must do more than put mine through the rinse cycle.

If I take the detergent to my brother's tunic, I had better add some softener.

I must not leave footprints on my brother's back just to prove I can get the dirt out in the wash.

Authorized version: It's hard to talk about judgment without sounding judgmental. Try it sometime.

I remember how one pastor criticized another who had resigned his church for health reasons. I remember the irreparable damage caused by that one man passing judgment on the other for the way he had "mismanaged" his church.

I remember a girl from a broken home, who just graduated from high school and planned to marry a "marginally committed," non-church guy. I know how discouraged that girl was when no one in the church seemed to understand her, though many freely judged her.

I remember a junior higher unhesitatingly reporting his parents' inconsistencies to the church youth group. Though the stories were not all true, the parents had a terrible reputation to live down in that church because of their son's judgmental spirit.

I remember a church that criticized its young people. I know how many left the church because of that. I also know what some of those kids are doing now, and how far they are from the Lord.

I have seen what the my-soap-your-laundry approach can do. Such a judgmental attitude can split a church, ruin a youth group, crush a person. And that's why it's hard to talk about judgment without being judgmental.

Some Christians Are All Teeth

Some Christians are famous for their cantankerous and sour dispositions. They're always talking about someone's shortcomings.

And some Christians are all teeth. But Paul cautioned: "You were called to freedom, brethren; only do not turn your freedom into an opportunity for the flesh, but through love serve one another. For the whole Law is fulfilled in one word, in the statement, 'You shall love your neighbor as yourself.' But if you bite and devour one another, take care lest you be consumed by one another" (Galatians 5:13-15).

Criticism looks ugliest on Christians.

Why do we so often wind up wearing it?

As Christians we are free, living life, Jesus-style. We have a strange new power to conquer bad habits and kiss the old life good-bye. We are

the light of the world, the salt of the earth.
Through Christ we have the capacity for a righteousness that surpasses that of the religious
leaders. We have our eyes on that lofty goal of
perfection.

Problem: It's so much easier to set that goal for
every other person we meet and establish a lower
standard for ourselves. So we check the wattage of
our brother's light and tell him, "That's no way to
light the world!" And we're not even plugged in.

We sample our brother's salt and complain,
"Blah! How bland can you get!" And we refuse to
let ours leave the salt shaker.

Paul said we have freedom in this new life, but
it is a freedom that must express itself in our
relationships with others. Back to the basics,
brothers! Do not use your freedom as an excuse for
sin. Serve one another in love. Don't be harsh and
critical. Love your neighbor.

That's exactly the point we have reached in the
Sermon. In our zeal for life, Jesus-style, we must
begin with *our* laundry. We correct *our* inconsistencies. We do not judge.

Judges Are a Dime a Baker's Dozen

"Do not judge," Jesus said, "lest you be judged
yourselves" (Matthew 7:1). And He gives three
reasons for not being hypercritical.

Number one: *If we judge others, we will be
judged.* The first reason He gives for not judging
others is that we will find ourselves being judged
if we do. He may be referring to the way God
breaks into a believer's life with judgment.

For example, we have mentioned in earlier
chapters God's judgment on Ananias and Sapphira (Acts 5:1-11). They were judged because

they lied to the church and to the Holy Spirit.

Paul told the church at Corinth that God had judged some of the believers for their conduct (1 Corinthians 11:29-32). As a result, some were sick, and some were dead.

The Apostle John said that there were some people who were committing a sin that led to death (1 John 5:16-17). God does judge believers.

So in a sense we invite the judgment of God when we persist in being critical and judgmental of others' lives. When we begin hurting the testimony of the church we need to look out. We may be a candidate for the judgment of God; not for heaven or hell, but for life or death; sickness or health.

But Jesus may be saying something even more basic. When we judge another person, we are likely to find that other person turning on us in judgment.

There is something about a critical spirit that breeds criticism in return. This may be one reason Jesus says, "Whatever you want others to do for you, do so for them; for this is the Law and the Prophets" (Matthew 7:12).

Jesus commands us to love others and leave the judging to God. That does not mean that we are to tolerate wrong or play up to sin (7:6). But whether we call our judgment "discernment," or "discretion," or whatever, we must exercise it in an atmosphere of love.

My own critical spirit haunts me. And I know from this passage of Scripture that I cannot easily dismiss this weakness.

Jesus was so perfectly balanced. He was meek, and patient with sinners. Yet He emptied the temple of its money-changers on two occasions, and He did it in anger (John 2:13-22; Matthew 21:12-13). He showed kindness and love for sinners who admitted their sinfulness. He had strong words of denunciation for religious hypocrites (Matthew 23).

For Sale Cheap: One Set of Used Balance Scales

Just in case we are not yet convinced that judgment is not part of our job descriptions as disciples, Jesus adds: "For in the way you judge, you will be judged; and by your standard of measure, it shall be measured to you" (Matthew 7:2).

Reason number two: *When we judge others, we set the standards for our own judgment.* If we judge others, we will be judged (7:1), and the standard of judgment will be the standard we set (7:2). That seems logical enough.

Again, we are confronted here with God's judgment—more severe for judgmental people. This is particularly true if we are committing the same offense that we are judging in someone else.

"Therefore you are without excuse, every man of you who passes judgment, for in that you judge another, you condemn yourself; for you who judge practice the same things" (Romans 2:1).

On the other hand, even if we are not committing the identical sin, we still condemn ourselves as we judge others. God sees His Law as a total package. If you break *any* point, you are a lawbreaker—guilty of violating the entire Law (James 2:10).

So James says, "Do not speak against one another, brethren. He who speaks against a brother, or judges his brother, speaks against the law, and judges the law; but if you judge the law, you are not a doer of the law, but a judge of it. There is only one Lawgiver and Judge, the One who is able to save and to destroy; but who are you who judge your neighbor?" (James 4:11-12)

It is also true that we set the standards for the way others judge us much of the time. Remember the story of Esther? Haman swung from the gallows he made for Mordecai (Esther 6—7). We often buy the party favors, hats, and whistles for our own necktie party.

We set the standards others will use to judge us, when we judge them.

You Always Hurt the One You Judge

"And why do you look at the speck in your brother's eye," Jesus asked, "but do not notice the log that is in your own eye?" (Matthew 7:3)

Talk about not seeing the forest for the trees! Log-man spends his time investigating reports of stray splinters finding their way into other people's eyes. But before he can complete an eye examination, he has clobbered the other guy with the tree protruding from his own eye.

Reason number three: *By judging others we demonstrate that we are not really qualified to judge at all.* The problem is inconsistency. We establish one set of values for the other guy and another one for ourselves.

Here is Log-man looking at Splinter-man, offering his assistance:

"I am an expert at locating splinters. Why I've found splinters in the best of 'em!"

And Splinter-man timidly replies: "Um, well, er, that's very nice of you . . . But, ah, about that pole . . ."

And a pole it was. Jesus used a word that was

used to describe the major beams in a house's construction and massive tree branches.

The point cannot be missed: Jesus is nailing people who are critical of sawdust sin while they are guilty of board-and-plank iniquity. But the specific sin that is being condemned is judgment.

Amazing How You Look When You See

"You hypocrite," Jesus continues, "first take the log out of your own eye, and then you will see clearly enough to take the speck out of your brother's eye" (Matthew 7:5).

Something refreshingly predictable happens when you get the log out of your eye: You can see. In fact, you can see so clearly that it is now possible to remove that speck from the other person's eye.

Notice that Jesus didn't say, "If you will only get that beam out of your eye, you'll really be able to see splinters in other people!" It's a fine point, but a crucial one. When the log is gone we can see clearly enough to *help*, not judge.

Paul said, "Brethren, even if a man is caught in any trespass, you who are spiritual, restore such a one in a spirit of gentleness; looking to yourself, lest you too be tempted" (Galatians 6:1).

As long as we are judging someone, we have not taken Jesus seriously. He said, "Do not judge, lest you be judged" (7:1).

We judge another person.

He judges us.

And we have enough weak areas for the other person to find. It becomes a standoff. He overlooks his own sin because he's reacting against our criticism.

Instead of helping the person we have hindered

him. We have given him another excuse to turn away from God. We have judged instead of loved.

But if we love the other person, without compromising our standard, we can become a powerful tool for the Holy Spirit to use. The person may come under God's judgment rather than ours, and he may have gotten his splinter removed.

I became a Christian in my teen years and I'm sure I've tripped other people up because I judged them. And judgment is something another person can often detect even if we never *say* anything. It bothers me to think that I have hurt a person's spiritual development by getting in the way of God's judgment, even if I have only made a silent judgment.

When we remove the log of our judgmental attitudes, then we are in a position to help others. And when we can *see* without criticizing, it's amazing how well we can look out for one another.

A Pig by Any Other Name Is Still a Pig

"Do not judge" does not mean "Do not think."

"Do not give what is holy to dogs, and do not throw your pearls before swine, lest they trample them under their feet, and turn and tear you to pieces" (Matthew 7:6).

We are cautioned about being too strict in judgment (Matthew 7:1-5). But now we are reminded not to be too lenient in our discernment.

God gives everybody, the good and the evil, His gifts of common grace—the sun, the rain. Every person is made in the image of God. He has dignity and ability, both gifts from God. But some things God reserves only for His family of believers.

We are not to give what is holy to "dogs." The

Bible applies this term, "dogs," to ungodly people. There will be no "dogs" in heaven—no ungodly people (Revelation 22:15). And Paul put up a sign in Philippians 3:2, "Beware of the dogs"—watch out for ungodly people.

Peter said, "A dog returns to its own vomit" (2 Peter 2:22). He was describing ungodly people, especially false teachers.

Jesus says, don't take the things that belong to God and toss them out to the ungodly. There are some things we can't share with unbelievers. They wouldn't know what to do with them.

And we are not to take our "pearls" and throw them before "swine." A pearl looks too much like a chunk of food. That hungry boar will charge right over to those pearls. But when he discovers it's not what he expected, he will whirl around and come at you with his tusks. If he can he'll rip you apart. And he will certainly trample those pearls under his feet.

As a dog returns to its vomit, "a sow, after washing, returns to wallowing in the mire" (2 Peter 2:22). Peter is referring to the ungodly again.

We are to be kind, generous, and loving toward all people, but we do not teach doctrine courses to people who will not appreciate them. We are not to expect the "natural man" to be able to understand the fine points of our Christianity (1 Corinthians 2:1-16). Nor are we to argue with people who love to be contentious (2 Timothy 2:23-26).

And talking about tossing pearls before swine, we should carefully think through the fad approach to Christianity—the Bubble-Saint approach. What does it really accomplish for Jesus to be known just by bumper stickers and slick slogans? Does it help Christianity? Or is it giving what is holy to dogs, and casting our pearls before swine?

Jesus was so perfectly balanced in all this. He taught people the truths of the Kingdom of God all day long. They listened; He taught. Yet He taught them in parables—"Seeing they do not see, and while hearing they do not hear, nor do they understand" (Matthew 13:13).

He patiently answered the questions of the rich man (Matthew 19:16-22), and of Nicodemus (John 3:1-21). But He often refused to answer the Pharisees, and refused to speak when He stood before Herod who had beheaded John the Baptist (Luke 23:8-9).

Throughout Jesus' ministry He carefully removed splinters from eyes, yet treated dogs as dogs, and pigs as pigs.

When we take our soap to our own laundry, God can use us as cleansing agents in our society. When we get the cumbersome logs out of our own eyes, we can see clearly enough to patiently lead others through the same steps to spiritual life. And as we do, we help others find life, Jesus-style.

11

You Say "Wet," I Say "Dry"

I've always had problems with prayer. First it was the now-I-lay-me-down-to-sleep routine. I wasn't sure what I meant when I said, "I pray the Lord my soul to keep. If I should die before I wake . . ." After all, wasn't I a bit young to be thinking about death? Talk about morbid!

I grew out of that problem and into some others What if John prays for rain, Sally prays for snow, Betty prays for fog, Herman prays for wind, and I pray for a sunny, calm day, all at the same time?

Take Old Testament Elijah for example. He is not as different from us as the years make him seem. James says, "Elijah was a man with a nature like ours" (5:17). If your nature is anything like mine, you know that James isn't handing out compliments.

Please know that I'm not selling Elijah short. I have deep respect for that man, and much to learn from him.

James continues, "He prayed earnestly that it might not rain; and it did not rain on the earth for three years and six months" (5:17).

Now then, don't you suppose that somewhere in all the land somebody must have been praying that it *would* rain? Perhaps some poor woman, who was watching her children die because of the famine and drought, was praying loudly for rain.

Maybe we all have a lot to learn about prayer.

Pigs, Poles, and Prayer

Jesus has some interesting things to say about prayer in the Sermon. In fact, it's the only point He discusses twice (6:5-15; 7:7-11).

In each of those two instances it helps to understand what He is talking about before He comes to the subject of prayer. Jesus says, "Beware of practicing your righteousness before men to be noticed by them; otherwise you have no reward with your Father who is in heaven" (6:1).

Then He gives three examples of practicing righteousness for show and tell: giving alms, prayer, and fasting. Each time Jesus mentions the wrong way, and then gives the right way. So He has already said several things about prayer:

Pray in secret (6:5-6). Don't do it for show. Prayer is fellowship with God, not entertainment for people.

Pray without empty repetition of words (6:7). God doesn't listen because we wear Him out. He listens because He wants to.

Pray in confidence (6:8). God knows our needs before we ask.

Pray for God's name to be honored (6:9). Celebrate His holiness.

Pray for God's big purposes (6:10). Ask for His kingdom; yield to His will.

Pray for daily needs (6:11). Not necessarily caviar, but not rocks instead of bread either.

Pray for forgiveness (6:12, 14-15). And tell God you are willing to forgive others.

Pray for strength in temptation (6:13). You need His help or you will fall on your face.

When Jesus picks up the prayer topic again (7:7-11) the context is just as important. Jesus urges, "Do not judge lest you be judged yourselves." He tells us to get the poles out of our eyeballs before investigating for splinters in other people's eyes (7:1-5).

But He also talks about the pork problem: "Do not throw your pearls before swine" (7:6). And be careful what you cast to the canines. Don't give holy things to dogs. Jesus is talking about the ungodly. It takes a certain amount of close observation to distinguish the ungodly from some believers.

So we find ourselves staring at an impossible standard. Life, Jesus-style: Be perfectly balanced. Discriminate, but do not judge.

But there may also be enough whimpy thread in us to tie us up in a sentimental, gutless accommodation to everybody. We will not judge; in fact we will tolerate anything and everything.

Jesus says we are to take a strong stand on right and wrong, but we are to do it lovingly. But we are *never* to pass judgment.

And the question comes: Where would we get a resource for that kind of response to people?

It is supernatural. It will not just happen. Even for Christians it will not just happen. We can't live life, Jesus-style, without a lot of help.

Ask, Seek, Knock

It is in that context that Jesus says, "Ask, and it shall be given to you; seek, and you shall find;

knock, and it shall be opened to you" (Matthew 7:7). See how abrupt the change is between this verse and the verses right before it? Jesus is trying to tell us something: There's help!

"Ask." We are to ask for God's help and keep on asking with a sense of complete dependence on Him. We believe He is there and eager to hear. And when we ask, He hears. "And it shall be given to you."

"Seek." Prayer is to be in earnest. As we ask God for gifts to meet our needs, so we seek those things He wishes to uncover—answers for our hassles. Many of our prayers are already answered in the Bible. And when we seek, He leads us to answers. "And you shall find."

"Knock." Talking to God gets active. Knocking has that sense of dependence that asking suggests, plus the earnestness that seeking implies. Here is that effort to reach out and hug God's promises. The idea is clear: We are so caught up by this request that we are banging on the door, even though we know God has already eagerly turned the knob to open it. And when we faithfully knock, He responds—always. "And it shall be opened to you."

So we ask, and keep on asking.

We seek, and keep on seeking.

We knock, and keep on knocking.

All because something is important to us.

"For everyone who asks receives, and he who seeks finds, and to him who knocks it shall be opened" (7:8).

What kind of person who sees people answer doors, or find lost things, or answer questions, would doubt God's ability to do the same in response to our prayers?

Hey Pop Could You Pass the Bread?

Maybe you've asked a service station attendant for directions and he told you to get lost. Or you dropped a five dollar bill, and somebody who wasn't even seeking, found it. Or you knocked on a friend's door till your knuckles bled and then a neighbor said, "They moved last week." With some people, asking, seeking, and knocking can be discouraging. But God is like a Father.

"What man is there among you, when his son shall ask him for a loaf, will give him a stone? Or, if he shall ask for a fish, he will not give him a snake, will he?" (Matthew 7:9-10)

Normal fathers do not keep good things from their children, nor do they substitute evil in place of good. When you ask for bread, your father doesn't give you bricks.

What kind of person can see fathers answering the requests of their children, treating them with love, tenderness, and concern, and still question God's interest in prayer and His ability to meet our needs?

Answer: A person who is more sure fathers exist than he is that *the* Father in heaven exists. A person who thinks fathers are kinder than God. "Dad gave me a Big Mac and fries. God I haven't seen."

Jesus is telling us, "If that's your concept of prayer, readjust it. It's wrong."

What if You Asked for Rocks, but Wanted Bread?

One bright afternoon in Southern California I took a brisk walk for a lunch break. I stopped at one of my favorite restaurants and ordered. I originally wanted to order a baconburger, medium.

But I asked for a mushroomburger, well done. The popularity of the odd little things had been mushrooming; I thought I should give them a fair try.

The sandwich was horrid! Those charbroiled mushrooms tasted just like ashes. Oh, that was vile! Obviously I'm not a mushroom fan anymore. I asked for something I did not want.

We often ask God for things that won't be good for us. But we don't have the sense to thank Him for saying, "No." God sees things from eternity's perspective. Between now and then our picture of the *real* world will change in drastic ways. I don't trust my judgment in prayer. I'm too dumb. I spend too much time asking for mushrooms. And the ones I think I want are probably just toadstools. I'm no connoisseur of life. God is.

"If you then, being evil, know how to give good gifts to your children, how much more shall your Father who is in heaven give what is good to those who ask Him!" (Matthew 7:11)

We are evil, naturally corrupt. Things just are not right on the inside. The theologians call it original sin. But in spite of our natural inclination toward evil, we can usually noodle our way through our other limitations and give our kids good gifts.

We are evil and give good gifts. God is good and gives fantastic gifts.

"How much more . . ." Jesus often appeals to an argument from the lesser to the greater. If parents will give good things, *how much more* will God do? Implied answer: Tons. Jesus says something similar when He compares God's care for birds with His care for us: "Are you not worth *much more* than they?" (6:26)

"Your Father who is in heaven . . ." Shades of

the Lord's Prayer. Remember, it was a new concept to talk to God as "Father" (6:8-9). And there's no chance that a *heavenly* Father will give something evil.

"Give what is good . . ." Jesus says, "If you then, being evil, know how to give good gifts to your children, how much more shall your heavenly Father give the Holy Spirit to those who ask Him?" (Luke 11:13)

God can give nothing better than the Holy Spirit, because in giving the Holy Spirit He is giving Himself.

Which Brings Us Back to the Original Question

Think of our friend Elijah again, and all those people who may have been praying that it would rain—that woman with her children dying of thirst. Also think of the Lord's model prayer: "Thy will be done, on earth as it is in heaven" (Matthew 6:10). What is more mysterious than God's will?

We can look back on Elijah and see part of the purpose of that prayer. The drought was a judgment for wickedness. Elijah, God's spokesman, was close enough to God to get a whiff of His purposes.

James' point in using Elijah's prayer as an example was to show us that fantastic things are not out of our reach. We can pray like Elijah did. We can believe as he did.

If Elijah had a middle name it was "Earnest." James sort of says so. Elijah prayed earnestly. We can claim the name, and the characteristic.

Go at it, Earnest!

But as you do, think it through. It's probably not God's will for you to ask Him to move the

Rocky Mountains to New Jersey, even if you *are* a ski fan! And there's really no great need for you to become the first 20th-century disciple to walk on water. Check out what you pray for. If you don't, the Holy Spirit will.

James said, "You do not have because you do not ask. You ask and do not receive, because you ask with wrong motives, so that you may spend it on your pleasures" (James 4:2-3). We can ask for the wrong things, in the wrong way, for the wrong purposes.

And then there are those things that seem for sure to be God's will. But nothing ever happens when we pray for them. And praying for those things gets tougher and tougher to do. God gives every Christian the Holy Spirit for that reason.

"And in the same way the Spirit also helps our weakness; for we do not know how to pray as we should, but the Spirit Himself intercedes for us with groanings too deep for words; and He who searches the hearts knows what the mind of the Spirit is, because He intercedes for the saints according to the will of God" (Romans 8:26-27).

In other words, the things we cannot adequately express, or we express wrong, the Holy Spirit communicates to the Father. And as the Holy Spirit does, He communicates our inadequate requests in terms of God's will. The Holy Spirit understands the Father's will because He is God. The Father—the One who searches hearts—knows the mind of the Spirit, because They are communicating on the same level. They are both Divine.

This explains, in part, why God gave such an incredible gift when He gave us the Spirit. The Spirit edits our prayers.

So We Give as He Gave

Matthew 7:12 is an important pivot point in the Sermon. When we hit that verse we have turned the corner and are headed straight toward the Lord's conclusion.

"Therefore whatever you want others to do for you, do so for them, for this is the Law and the Prophets."

At the beginning of the Sermon, Jesus said, "Do not think that I came to abolish the Law or the Prophets." And He summarizes the teaching of Matthew 7:1-11, the entire Sermon, and the Old Testament in one verse.

We are not to judge (7:1-5), but we must be discerning (7:6). God will help us (7:7-11). But when it comes down to a face-to-face, eyeball-to-eyeball relationship, how do I act toward another person? There's only one answer: Seek his highest good.

We are to be the salt of the earth, the light of the world, with a righteousness surpassing that of the religious leaders. And, in a capsule, how must all that express itself? There's still only one answer: Seek the highest good of the other person.

Other religious leaders and philosophers have said similar things, but no one said precisely this.

Hillel said, "Do not do to thy neighbor what is hateful to thyself."

Socrates said, "What stirs your anger when done to you by others that do not to others."

Aristotle improved on it: "We should bear ourselves toward others as we would desire they should bear themselves toward us."

Or Confuscius, "What you do not want done to yourself do not do to others."

This is a hard enough standard. But they are all

negative. If you do not like being mugged, don't mug. But Jesus throws it all in the positive. Do not sit back passively, not doing bad things to people you meet. Instead, run on into life actively pursuing good for others, forgetting yourself.

That is the Law and the Prophets.

Forgetting yourself is impossible without a lot of help. So ask, and keep on asking. Seek, and keep on seeking. Knock, and keep on knocking.

Then thank God for His answer: life, Jesus-style.

"ADAM'S APPLE" WAS THE START OF SOMETHING VERY UNFORTUNATE: FELLOWSHIP WITH GOD WAS DAMAGED TO THE CORE.

12

Adam's Apple and the Human Core

I sat on the roof of my friend's 1952 Ford with my feet resting on the hood. I was holding a pair of bongos between my legs, pounding out a rhythm to accompany the blaring car radio.

Four of us were just pulling into the church parking lot for the Sunday evening service. And as we cruised slowly around that parking lot, we got the congregation's attention.

We gave our pastor fits. Yet something kept us going back to that church. And something kept our pastor working with us.

When, as a graduating high school senior, I finally let Christ help me get my life together, that pastor told my mom, "I would have believed it about anybody but Jim!"

Touché, Preacher.

Throughout my four years of high school I trusted an emotional religious experience to get me into heaven if I should die. Admittedly, getting into heaven was a small chance.

Yet I did think about dying occasionally, like the time we had been pulled over by the Califor-

143

nia Highway Patrol for racing down the Pacific Coast Highway at 100 mph, but were released when the officer got an emergency call. And we saw that emergency call just a few miles down the road. It was a flattened wreckage of a car so crushed that it wasn't much more than waist-high. That driver had been speeding too.

When I thought about eternity I wondered, with all my churchgoing and my religious experience, was I really a Christian?

But those thoughts are easy to chase out of your mind, especially when you are afraid of what your friends will think.

Broad Road, Narrow Road

Young Christians are generally steered toward the Gospel of John. And John 3:16 is about the first thing they memorize. But I broke the mold. The first verse I memorized as a child was Matthew 7:12:

"Therefore all things whatsoever ye would that men should do to you, do ye even so to them: for this is the law and the prophets" (King James Version).

The second passage that I memorized was the Lord's Prayer (Matthew 6:9-13).

For that reason Matthew has always been sort of special to me. When I turned to a Gospel, it was usually Matthew. I became familiar with Matthew 7:13-14 long before I turned to Christ.

Those verses always haunted me—especially during those occasional times when I thought about death or eternity.

"Enter by the narrow gate; for the gate is wide, and the way is broad that leads to destruction, and many are those who enter by it. For the gate is small, and the way is narrow that leads to life, and few are those who find it" (Matthew 7:13-14).

Taken seriously, these are disturbing words. Somehow they just don't convey the same image as the pink-cheeked, mild-mannered, Clark Kent type Jesus that is sometimes pictured. There is intensity in those words, a sense of urgency.

Those verses violated my image of gentle Jesus, meek and mild. Here was a Jesus who expected a lot from me; a Jesus who laid out the life and death issues.

But I was too busy struggling with being accepted by the group "now," "today." Instead Jesus was talking about acceptance with God, going against the group. He was talking about that Ultimate Tomorrow, judgment. And it bothered me.

Yet I compromised my actions and beliefs when the pressures from the group, and my own drive for acceptance, got too much. And I just kept putting Jesus off; always with the nagging sensation, *This isn't quite right. This is that broad road. Does it really lead to destruction?*

A Proverbs writer expresses the same thought. "There is a way which seems right to a man, but its end is the way of death" (14:12). So important is that concept that it is repeated word for word two chapters later (16:25).

There is something hideously precarious about following the broad road. We find that it's broad enough for secular-minded people, broad-minded people, and all religious people. It's broad enough for everyone but Jesus.

I was thinking of that broad road and the people who were listening to His Sermon. They were quite religious, particularly when compared with most Americans, for example.

Jesus began the Sermon talking to His disciples on the mountainside (Matthew 5:1-2). But by the time He completed the Sermon there was a massive crowd listening to Him (7:28—8:1). Some of them were grossly immoral I guess, but many of them were probably "good," devout Jews.

And Jesus seems to be telling that basically religious mob the same thing He told them earlier: "Your righteousness just has to exceed the righteousness of your religious leaders. They are on the broad road, and it leads to destruction."

This sensation—that it was not enough to go to church, to be religious—bothered me a great deal throughout my high school years. I was going to church, driving the preacher nuts, trusting a vague I-raised-my-hand/I-walked-the-aisle religious experience to get me into heaven. But I was on the broad road, going to hell.

The Tale of Two Preachers . . .
One Was Forked

Different people respond differently to the narrowness of Jesus. One preacher told me, "I don't see how anyone could be so egotistical to say he's found the only way." He was referring to John 14:6. At the time I wanted to punch his lights out, call down fire from heaven.

Then another preacher, sort of everybody's dad type guy, confessed, "They tell me I'm so narrow I could sleep in a macaroni."

Well, I'll vote for Preacher Number Two—Macaroni Man. The narrowness of Jesus never really bothered me. I always figured that if truth was narrow, *The* Truth was certainly entitled to be.

What did bother me, though, were the demands

of that narrowness, knowing that taking the narrow gate, the narrow road, would involve a tremendous sacrifice. And I wasn't sure I was willing
to give it a go.

I would have to admit that I was wrong; Jesus
was right. My values were selfish; His were godly.
My direction led to destruction; His to life.
Strange, isn't it, that so few people find that narrow gate, life: Jesus-style.

"And if it is with difficulty that the righteous is
saved, what will become of the godless man and
the sinner?" (1 Peter 4:18)

But the problem is still more complicated. Even
if I decide to take the narrow way, people will
always be trying to turn me around and put me
back on the broad road.

I used to think of these two ways as if there was
some obvious fork in the road, sort of a you-take-
the-high-road-and-I'll-take-the-low-road   approach. Now I wonder if that narrow road isn't
right in the middle of that broad road, going the
opposite direction. In some ways I think it is.

And any person who decides to live life, Jesus
style, must realize that he will be jostled by the
crowds. And friends and enemies and religious
leaders will grab him by the shoulders and try to
whirl him around and point him once again toward destruction.

"Beware of the false prophets," Jesus said, "who
come to you in sheep's clothing, but inwardly are
ravenous wolves" (Matthew 7:15).

Here's the judgment/discernment theme again.
In order to beware of false teachers, I must make
a judgment. I must discern who they are. And
Jesus tells me to look at their characters, examine
their lives.

"You will know them by their fruits. Grapes are not gathered from thornbushes, nor figs from thistles, are they? Even so every good tree bears good fruit; but the rotten tree bears bad fruit. A good tree cannot produce bad fruit, nor can a rotten tree produce good fruit. Every tree that does not bear good fruit is cut down, and thrown into the fire. So then, you will know them by their fruits" (Matthew 7:16-20).

So false teachers are like ravenous wolves— worse than dogs, worse than hogs (7:6). And false teachers are like corrupt, rotten trees that sprout bad fruit. Sometimes they are bad teachers, teaching bad things. Sometimes they say all the right things. They may even agree with my theology, but their lives are wrong.

They preach, teach, witness, talk—all for the wrong motives of pride and power. But I just can't copy their lives. They aren't living Jesus-style.

Earth-Prone/Now-Oriented

We don't usually choose mean people for close friends. If somebody harms us, we usually make a mental note: "He slugged me in the mouth. My mouth hurt intensely, my lip bled, my jaw swelled. Stay away from this guy."

Isn't it a bit weird, though, that we figure we haven't been hurt much if we are OK physically? We are so earth-prone/now-oriented we see life with shades of today and that's all. We won't tolerate somebody repeatedly hurting us physically, but somebody can almost destroy us spiritually and we go back for more and more and more.

Look how many guy-girl relationships devastate people's spiritual lives. But there's usually little willingness to break these relationships

WE ARE SO EARTH-PRONE/NOW-ORIENTED
WE SEE LIFE IN SHADES OF TODAY
AND THAT'S ALL.

SO WE GAIN OUR WORLDS OF
ACCEPTANCE, AND LOSE OUR SOULS.

OR WE GAIN OUR WORLDS OF
GOOD TIMES, BUT FORFEIT
OUR LIVES.

We will tolerate most anything—friendships, drug and alcohol involvement, habits—no matter how much they cost us spiritually. We don't want to be different. So we gain our worlds of acceptance, and lose our souls. Or we gain our worlds of good times, but forfeit our lives.

There are people who will make entering the narrow gate and keeping on that narrow road more difficult. Jesus tells us to avoid those people at all costs.

He warns us about a lot of things that will divide our attentions and hinder our lives. He uses that word, "Beware" (Matthew 6:1), cautioning us to avoid seeing righteousness as a show we perform for people.

Adam's Apple and the Human Core

What we are on the inside will express itself on the outside.

Jesus illustrates the point with grapes and figs, thorns and thistles (7:16). He states plainly that good trees bear good fruit; bad trees bear bad fruit (7:17). Then He says it negatively, bad trees do not give good fruit; good trees do not give bad fruit (7:18).

This whole evil-root problem can be traced on humanity's family tree right back to Adam's apple. Chomping down on the Golden Delicious, disobeying the only restriction he had been given, affected the entire human core.

Because of that, till we begin life, Jesus-style, till we get His new life in our core, we are not capable of producing good fruit. So as we stand, looking at that narrow road and wondering, we not only have the problem of others who would lead us astray. We also have our own hearts, which the Bible says are so wicked we cannot even know them ourselves (Jeremiah 17:9).

"Not everyone who says to Me, 'Lord, Lord,' will enter the kingdom of heaven; but he who does the will of My Father, who is in heaven" (Matthew 7:21).

This is right doctrine. Jesus is acknowledged as Lord. A hand has been raised. An aisle has been walked. A prayer has been offered. But something isn't quite right. There was an intellectual, "Yes, Jesus is Lord," but it didn't penetrate the entire core. There was not a changed life (2 Corinthians 5:17). James said even the demons "believe, and shudder" (James 2:19). They believe, but there's no change.

The sincerity of the words "Lord, Lord" is tested by a desire to do God's will. Is there a new value system? Is there *life,* Jesus-style? Or just words?

"Many will say to Me on that day, 'Lord, Lord, did we not prophesy in Your name, and in Your name cast out demons, and in Your name perform many miracles?' And then I will declare to them, 'I never knew you; depart from Me, you who practice lawlessness'" (Matthew 7:22-23).

All the sermons preached by hypocrites, all the witnessing done by people who weren't Christians, all the miracles and tongues performed or babbled by not-genuine people amount to nothing.

And Jesus will openly declare, "Though I saw you and was aware of your motives, though I heard you use My name, though a lot of people were impressed by your flashy spiritual stuff, your Bible reading and your prayer, I never knew you. Good-bye. You turned the practice of righteousness into lawlessness."

I know that's a lot of heavy, serious stuff to think about. But somehow, during my high school years, John 3:16 did not keep me awake at night. I glossed right over it. I just turned up the music, pounded the drums a bit louder, and got the attention of the church, hoping that somebody would say, "Hey, you're all right."

But there were those times, just a bit too frequent, when I thought about life, and death, and eternity, and Matthew 7, and I was disturbed.

Until I found life, Jesus-style.

13

Same Song, Same Stanza

I have this thing about Gospel songs. I already mentioned that. But here I am, again pondering that same ol' chorus:

> *I've got a home in glory land*
> *that outshines the sun . . .*
> *Away beyond the blue . . .*

I am still thinking that my revised version is for most of us, more honest:

> *I've got a home in glory land,*
> *But my feet are firm on this here sod,*
> *Dear God!*

Oh are they ever firm!

But Jesus is telling us over and over and over again, our values must be made in heaven. We are just visitors here.

Life, Jesus-style, begins when we realize that all we've ever known of life is not life at all. That's why we are invited to enter a narrow gate and hike a narrow road that leads to *life* (Matthew 7:13-14).

My image of heaven, at the end of that narrow road, does not involve a lot of harp playing. (I'd

rather have a guitar.) But a big part of my image of heaven is this:

We are finally going to get the full picture of life from God's perspective. Jesus preached the Sermon on the Mount because He doesn't want us to be too surprised when we get there.

God's values are so counter to our nature. But He wants us to live this earthly life, Jesus-style, so that our transition into that life is smooth and joyous.

And the Rains Came a-Tumblin' Down

Children's songs are sometimes a bit misleading. For example, it's hard to read Matthew 7:24-27 without visualizing a mob of five-year-olds, standing on the platform of the church. Half of them are looking around. A mischievous tow-headed kid is pulling the hair of the girl next to him. And a nice middle-aged lady with a loud voice is directing them.

The kids pound their fists together and wiggle their little pinkies as they sing, "The wise man built his house upon the rock." And even when they come to the crash of the foolish man's house, and shout out those words with such energy, still we are left with the feeling of how cute that little ditty was.

But what Jesus said wasn't cute at all.

"Therefore everyone who hears these words of Mine, and acts upon them, may be compared to a wise man, who built his house upon the rock. And the rain descended, and the floods came, and the winds blew, and burst against that house; and yet it did not fall, for it had been founded upon the rock

"And everyone who hears these words of Mine,

and does not act upon them, will be like a foolish man, who built his house upon the sand. And the rain descended, and the floods came, and the winds blew, and burst against that house; and it fell, and great was its fall" (Matthew 7:24-27).

So as Jesus had given a contrast between a broad road and a narrow road, and between a bad tree and a good tree, He now contrasts two buildings. One building has a sand foundation, the other a rock foundation. Though both buildings look solid on sunny summer days, the two withstand adversity with quite different levels of success.

Can you visualize a sudden rainstorm, the flash floods, the Jordan River swelling, and finally overflowing its banks? The man who has haphazardly thrown together a shack on the side of the riverbank is inviting problems. Big problems. Wet problems.

So Jesus gave this vivid picture of two lives. We have a man who does a decent job putting his life together. The other man just has not figured out life at all. The element Jesus gives that makes the difference is this Sermon.

The Sermon is the issue. He's talking to people who just heard it, and He is now saying, "what are you going to do about it?"

Rome Is Not the Only Thing that Wasn't Built in a Day

I've already mentioned that I had a vague religious experience the summer after I graduated from junior high—Dinky Creek, High Sierras, California. And, like a bad vaccination, it didn't "take." My four years of high school were less than exhilarating, spiritually speaking.

But, as a high school senior, things did begin to fit together spiritually. And that's when the changes started happening. I found life, Jesus-style, and having found it, I have never been the same.

Instant sainthood? Well . . . Rome isn't the only thing that wasn't built in a day. Disneyland used to advertise with a little slogan something like, "As long as there is imagination, Disneyland will never be completed." The Lord is a bit more creative than the Disney people.

"For we are His workmanship, created in Christ Jesus for good works, which God prepared beforehand, that we should walk in them" (Ephesians 2:10). That's the way Paul expressed it.

I find it interesting the way the Sermon portrays life, Jesus-style. It is a narrow gate, a narrow way to life (Matthew 7:13-14). It is not just a narrow gate we step through and it's all over. We step through the gate—we're in, we have it—but then we walk that narrow road. It's something we *begin* and *continue*.

We also get the picture of two trees, two fruits (7:16-20). If we have life, Jesus-style, we are good trees, producing good fruit. But trees, good or bad, are *continuing* to produce fruit.

Then Jesus tells us life is like two buildings (7:24-27). The building is erected to stand and be useful, it has a *continuing* purpose. As it stands and serves as a home or whatever, it is subjected to the test of time, the severity of storms.

I sense that Jesus is letting us know there is a resource to keep us going on that narrow road to life. There is a plant food that will keep us blooming and producing that good fruit. There is a solid, enduring rock that will serve as a foundation to keep our building stable, continuing to stand. That foundation is His Word.

When life, Jesus-style, finally began making sense to me, I practically turned my room into a monastery. I started spending every available coin on Christian books—and I made some dumb purchases; I bought some books I still haven't read. But there were some wise purchases too. They helped me grow and continue following Jesus, rather than sitting down on the narrow road, or skipping entire seasons of fruit-bearing, or turning my building into a run-down shack.

Church took on a new significance, which, quite frankly, surprised me at the time. My friendships began to change. And I wanted to share life, Jesus-style, with others. My language changed—drastically. Some habits dropped off, others frustrated me because I had difficulty shaking them.

The changes came excruciatingly slow. But they did come. Even though I tripped over my own feet—and sometimes my shadow—I was walking that narrow road to life. Even though I shook off some of my own fruit long before it was ripe, and tried to graft on some bad limbs, Jesus had made me a good tree with an increasing crop of good fruit. Even though I opened the doors and windows in the middle of a few floods, my building was set on a good solid rock foundation.

I found life, Jesus-style.

No Closing Hymn, No Final Benediction

"Therefore everyone who hears these words of Mine, and acts upon them, may be compared to a wise man, who built his house upon the rock. And the rain descended, and the floods came, and the winds blew, and burst against that house; and yet it did not fall, for it had been founded upon the rock.

"And everyone who hears these words of Mine, and does not act upon them, will be like a foolish man, who built his house upon the sand. And the rain descended, and the floods came, and the winds blew, and burst against that house; and it fell, and great was its fall" (Matthew 7:24-27).

Zap! Just like that the Sermon was over. No closing hymn. No final benediction. And just like that house collapsed and fell with a great crash, Jesus demolished the false security of trusting goodness that was generated by human effort.

Righteousness must surpass that of the religious leaders.

We must be perfect as our heavenly Father is perfect.

And the house fell, and great was its fall.

"The result was that when Jesus had finished these words, the multitudes were amazed at His teaching; for He was teaching them as one having authority, and not as their scribes. And when He had come down from the mountain, great multitudes followed Him" (Matthew 7:28—8:1).

The entire Sermon had been carefully calculated to present God's impossible standard—life, Jesus-style. In presenting that impossible standard, those who heard were to sense the need for Someone who could fulfill the Law and the Prophets—all of God's demands. That's the reason for Christ's crucifixion and resurrection—He paid for our inability to meet the standard.

The Sermon on the Mount then, shows us our need to trust Christ, accepting His special gift of *eternal* life But that's only the beginning. His

Holy Spirit comes in to help us make the Word our foundation for life, Jesus-style.

It's fine to sing about our home in glory land, way beyond the blue. But we'd better live like we have one, so our feet are not too firm on this here sod. Because if we get too comfortable in our home here, with our values oriented to this life only, we may deceive ourselves.

And the rains will descend, and the floods will come, and the winds will blow, and burst against our houses. And they may fall with a great cosmic crash.